GOLDEN *Lily*

Making Waves

The real lives of sporting heroes on, in & under the water

Also in this series...

The First Indian
by Dilip Donde

The story of the first Indian solo circumnavigation under sail

more to follow

GOLDEN *Lily*

Lijia Xu

Edited by Jeremy Atkins

FERNHURST
BOOKS

A catalogue record for this book is available from the British Library
ISBN 978-1-909911-47-5

Photography
All photographs supplied by Lijia Xu, except:
p12 (top) © Paul Gilham/Staff; p14, p15 (top) © Clive Mason/Staff; p15 (bottom) ©
Rolex/Kurt Arrigo; p16 (top) © BMW AG; p16 (bottom) © Rick Tomlinson/Team SCA

p12 contains text from *Close to the Wind* by Ben Ainslie, published by Yellow Jersey.
Reproduced by permission of The Random House Group Ltd.

p142 contains text from *Wild Swans* by Jung Chang. Reprinted by permission of
HarperCollins*Publishers* and Jung Chang © 1991 Jung Chang.

Designed by Rachel Atkins
Printed in the UK by Clays Ltd, St Ives plc

Contents

Foreword

by Sir Ben Ainslie

Lijia Xu (Lily, as those of us in the west know her) is a true sailing champion. To date she has won the Optimist Girls World Championship twice, the Laser Radial Women's World Championship and a gold medal in the 2012 London Olympic Games, as well as many other Regional and National Titles.

This impressive list makes her an inspiration for sailors, particularly female sailors, around the world. But, as this fascinating autobiography reveals, there is far more to Lily than the medals she has won.

Brought up in a country and region without a strong competitive sailing heritage, Lily was the first ever Asian dinghy gold medallist. To achieve this, she had to supplement the Chinese emphasis on relentless training with help from outside China to really hone her sailing skills. On top of this, she had to overcome inherited physical frailties and career threatening injuries.

Golden Lily is an enthralling account of Lily's life, whilst also being a fascinating eye-opener into the Chinese sports 'machine', where people like Lily become professional sportspeople at the age of 10, shedding light on the reality of growing up as a state sponsored child athlete.

Lily and I shared many precious memories in 2012. We both

won sailing gold medals, we both carried our country's national flag at the Olympic Closing Ceremony and we were both voted ISAF Rolex World Sailors of the Year.

I have nothing but respect for Lily. I commend this book to anyone interested in sailing, sport or the differences between east and west.

Sir Ben Ainslie, 2016

Prologue

Before I start my story, let me pick some English names for my Chinese coaches and team members to help you recognise and remember them:

Lily   My English name
Juliet My Optimist coach with the Shanghai Sailing Team
Echo   An Optimist sailor who then moved to the Laser Radial
Lima   Head coach of the Chinese Olympic Sailing Team
Zulu   Team leader of the Chinese Olympic Sailing Team
Yankee Former team leader before Zulu
Quebec Director of the Chinese Yachting Association
Golf   Team doctor

As well as my personal story, dotted throughout the book are 'interludes' where I share my thoughts on some aspects of being a professional sportswoman and 'positive affirmations' which I wrote during my career. I pinned these positive affirmations up on my wall and read them every day. They helped to shape my success. The most precious one is the one I wrote one year before the London Olympics about what it felt like to be the Olympic Champion (p103). Be positive and dreams do come true!

Chapter 1

Golden Lily

"One day you will wake up and it is 30th July". (This date was the first day of racing for the Laser Radial class in the London 2012 Olympic Games.)

This was a sentence my English coach, Jon Emmett, said to me one year before the London Olympics, and he kept on repeating it every now and again. He was trying to help me prepare for this feeling at the start of this big event. And now it was here!

Since there was limited accreditation for each team, only Lima was registered as my coach and Jon wasn't even able to enter the Olympic Venue or Athletes' Village. My Chinese mobile phone and laptop had been confiscated by the team, just as it had been in the last Olympic Games in Qingdao. My coaches and leaders believed that I would be protected from pressure and distraction if I was not able to contact anyone in China during the event.

Fortunately I could still use my UK phone and keep up communication with Jon. He had set his own phone on 'outdoor mode' 24 hours a day during the Olympics and I knew that I could always speak to him, day or night. Every morning I would receive detailed e-mails from Jon with that day's analysis of the weather, course area, race strategy and key words I needed to remember. Then I would give him a call for a short conversation, instead of a face-to-face meeting, before heading to the venue. He would always end the call with a few final positive words, like "I believe in you"; "We strive to do our very best, hand in hand"; "Let us make the most of the Games"; "Work hard and have fun"; "Every day, in every way, I get better and better"; and so on.

After racing we would meet in the gym, doing some light aerobics, followed by a deep stretch to help my body recover quicker. In order to make it less obvious, Jon borrowed his mother's car, rather than driving his van which had a big logo saying 'Jon Emmett Sailing' on it. As usual, we used that time to do our debrief, but this week it was more about psychological topics than sailing.

As Ben Ainslie put in his book, *Close to the Wind*: "I was nervous that first day for sure. I don't think you'd be human if you didn't show some nerves." If even the greatest sailing legend in the world gets nervous, how could I not miss the occasional heart beat? Yes, I had times of stress as well.

Armed with my experience from the last Olympics, I didn't resist it. Instead, I acknowledged it and welcomed the fact that every competitor was under a certain pressure, big or small. What matters is how you deal with it and still perform the best you can. Indeed, all my effort went into controlling the pressure, and I just raced with my subconscious mind. This is where mental visualisation plays a crucial role. By visualising over and over again, I created the perfect image in my memory bank, so that I could perform effortlessly without thinking about it, since it was already second nature to me.

On the first day of racing, I got a fifth and eighth, and was lying fifth overall. I felt my approach and style was too conservative and wasn't really stretching my sailing fully. Part of the reason for this was that I used to be frequently scored OCS (on the course side) or BFD (black flagged for being over the start line), resulting in disqualification from the race. I am very good at positioning myself at the favoured end of the starting line, but it is the riskiest place to be. It is a double-edged sword: most of the time I would be among the leading group from right after the start to the finish, but it has also cost me many championships over the years. In the 2007, 2008, 2009, 2011 and 2012 Women's Laser Radial World Championships I was disqualified in at least one race because of this. Apart from 2011 in Perth, I was so close to many World Championships which I didn't win for this reason. The cost is so high that I decided to play it safe in the Olympics. I would rather start conservatively, with the chance of catching up later, than get an OCS and be completely out of contention.

Annalise Murphy, from Ireland, had a brilliant start to the Games, scoring four first places in a row. After two days' racing I was 23 points behind Annalise and in fifth place. From the third day onwards, I consistently climbed up the leader board every day, and entered the final Medal Race with the yellow (leader's) bib.

This race was going to be a fierce competition. Of the top four sailors (Lijia Xu, China; Marit Brouwmeester, Netherlands; Annalise Murphy, Ireland; Evi Van Acker, Belgium): whoever won the Medal Race would be the Olympic Champion. It had been a pretty dramatic series as all the medal hopes had had some ups and downs – and after ten races we would start even again, for possibly the most important race in all our lives.

The intense atmosphere made it feel difficult to breathe, and

I am sure many others, from all over the world, experienced a sleepless night, whether they were sailors, families, friends, coaches, leaders, fans or sponsors.

I spent most of my spare time before the race using visualisation. I went through the perfect race in my mind over and over again, in vivid detail, as if I was actually sailing on the sea, experiencing the scene, the sound, the smell and the feel. I imagined myself as an elegant actress, facing millions of spectators and live TV viewers, thousands of home supporters, hundreds of journalists and dozens of cameras. I was going to give my best performance to the whole world!

In between my mental visualisation I would switch on the music, set to replay one song which best suited the scenario at that special moment, singing along to relax myself:

> *Got sun in my eyes*
> *Got wind in my sails*
> *The future at my feet*
> *The best in life is yet to come cos I believe*
> *I'm givin' it all for joy*
> *I'm givin' it everything with all my heart*
> *I'm givin' it all to prove*
> *You never know your limit*
> *When the passion drives you*
> *All for joy*
> *I'm aiming for better than the best I've got*
> *I'm givin' it all to prove*
> *You never know your limit, power is inside you*

(All For Joy, © Lyricist: Sharon Kwan; Composer: David Tao)

I heard this song performed in a stadium at an event organised by my sponsor, BMW, earlier in 2012. It was written specially for BMW and the launch of their support of the Olympic Games. At first I was just attracted by the melody as I couldn't hear the words clearly. Immediately after the event, I searched for the name of the song, downloaded it and looked closely at those words and what they meant. Wow, it was as if it was written for me! It was such a happy discovery and later it became the theme tune of my London Olympic Games. My final race strategy was that simple: ALL FOR JOY! "I am giving it everything with all of my heart!" I sang loudly with the music.

In the last briefing with Jon he told me to sail my own race and follow my instinct. He reminded me that, as far as Rule 42 (making the boat go faster through certain actions like pumping, rocking or sculling) was concerned, there was a different penalty in the Medal Race from the rest of the regatta. Usually when you are first whistled for breaking Rule 42, you have to do two turns, and the second time it happens in a regatta you have to retire from the race. I already had received one penalty in the regatta, so normally another one in this race would mean I would have to retire from the Medal Race, with no chance of a medal. But it is different for the Medal Race and every whistle means 'just' a two turn penalty.

Jon carefully checked that day's forecast and observed that there might be some shifts to the right. His final words on the phone were "sail like a new regatta and embrace every challenge". Jon made me laugh several times that morning, making me feel happy and relaxed. He knew it was going to be a good day, but didn't know just how good.

Before launching, every sailor had to go through the media

zone for interviews. As it says in the song, I said that I was going to give it all for joy, with all of my heart. When each of us spoke you could almost hear our coaches' words, as they had repeatedly said some key words to us. This was true for me, Marit and Evi, although Annalise did not appear in front of the camera; it was her coach who did the interview for her.

The conditions for our Medal Race were very different to the previous ones. The wind had been lighter for the previous Medal Races and the left hand side of the beat had been favoured. For our race, there was still more wind on the left, but because the wind was stronger, the extra pressure would not give more speed. Jon advised me that the shifts on the right (near the land) would be more important.

I asked Jon how windy it was and he assured me it wouldn't be too windy as the wind would be strongest for the Men's Laser Medal Race after ours. Thank goodness we had our Medal Race before the wind increased.

I launched an hour before the starting time as usual. I did my normal pre-race routine and everything was well planned. It was a westerly wind of 12-15 knots. The Medal Race was held on the Nothe course area, where it could be very shifty since it was close to the shore. After checking the course three times (upwind and downwind), and tracking the wind for about 30 minutes, I found out that there was always a wind bend on the right hand side, but more wind on the left, upwind.

Before starting, Lima told me that, based on past data on this area and in this wind direction, the left hand side had a higher ratio of winning upwind. Meanwhile, the starting line was biased towards the pin end (left hand side) by about 15 degrees. Now I had to make the decision about which side of the course I was going to sail, based on this information about this tricky area.

In the end, I chose to start by the pin end (left hand side) and tack onto port (to go right) at the first opportunity, to take advantage of the wind bend on the right hand side upwind. I would then sail high after rounding the windward mark to get the left hand side gusts on the run (which would actually be the right hand side downwind).

I had a so-so start as I managed to position myself as the second boat next to the leeward end (pin), but my acceleration wasn't good enough. Within a minute, I was overtaken by Marit (NED) who was the third boat by the pin.

"No problem, Lily, I can now tack onto port and head for the right hand side of the course", I said to myself and did so. But I was then almost last as I had to duck (sail behind) all the right-of-way boats on starboard. Despite this temporary loss, I actually felt more confident heading to the right because I was on the best lift (or heading) on port. This meant that all the starboard boats were sailing lower than the average heading, because of the oscillating wind shift to the left.

It was risky because the majority of the fleet were sailing to the left and only two boats were on the right. If my judgement turned out to be wrong, then my game was over – I would be off the podium, or certainly not on the top of it. However, my port tack angle was so high that I was convinced that I should continue on this route without any hesitation.

As I anticipated, the wind started to shift back to the right before I reached the lay line (the course to round the mark). I tacked immediately and the wind kept veering, taking me up all the way to the first mark. I was second after crossing all the other boats. Annalise (IRL) was leading the fleet and she was, no doubt, the fastest upwind in medium to strong winds.

After rounding the windward mark I sailed to the right, as I had intended, to stay in the best wind pressure, and soon overtook the Irish boat. Suddenly I heard a whistle coming from behind. Looking back, a judge was pointing a yellow flag at me and hailed "China"! I was being penalised for breaking Rule 42. It is strange that I have rarely been whistled and got a yellow flag, but did in my two Olympic Games. I am a very smooth sailor and struggle to do manoeuvres aggressively, whereas Marit and Evi's combative sailing styles have led to them having had several whistles from the judges (including at this Olympics).

Well, it wasn't going to matter since Jon had reminded me that it did not mean a retirement in the Medal Race and I had imagined so many times how to deal with different types of on-the-water incidents. I didn't even waste a moment to reflect on what had happened or what went wrong. Instead, I accepted it, dealt with it, let it go and promptly focussed back on my race. Watching the live TV ashore, Jon was also relieved that he had reminded me I did not have to retire and was pleased to see me take the penalty quickly.

This approach was deeply rooted in my subconscious and I reacted quickly with a penalty turn and then concentrated on my downwind steering again. I was completely unaware of my position at that point and it was not until I watched the video on shore afterwards that I realised that I had dropped from first to fourth place. It seems that I was wholly engaged in my own race and didn't bother to think about anything that was beyond my control. I don't know how I passed the other three boats to be leading again, but we were all very close to each other.

Before rounding the leeward mark, GBR and NED attempted

to get an overlap inside me (and so have the right to go inside me at the mark) by sailing much higher than the lay line to the mark. I luffed firmly not to give them any chances.

*

It is worth mentioning a story linked to this successful tactical execution. It happened one day when we were sailing in Dongshan (China). I encountered a similar scenario and sailed 'kindly' to let my teammate establish an inside overlap. Afterwards Jon stopped his boat and talked to me earnestly for half an hour about my wrong attitude. I said to him "why take it so seriously since it is only a training session". That day he made me never forget that situation and the principle of treating every training experience as real racing. And now that little talk, and my confident implementation, was going to help decide the outcome of an Olympic Games!

*

Going back to my final race, I managed to protect my leading position all the way to the finish by combining tactics with playing the shifts. At the finish line I couldn't help myself and shouted loudly and raised my arm to celebrate my victory. I kissed my boat and thanked her for her cooperation and company on this wonderful journey.

Marit (NED) was next, following about 30 metres behind, and claimed the silver medal. Evi (BEL) was the third finisher in that Medal Race and got a bronze overall.

For the first time in my life, Lima and Quebec hugged me to

celebrate when I approached the coaches' RIB. I could hardly conceal my excitement, raising and waving the Chinese flag high up with the sail. Wow – I had made history: the first ever sailing dinghy gold medal for both China and Asia! I was the shiniest 'actress' that day and I succeeded in presenting my very best 'show' to the whole world. Lily rocks!

Jon was not given a ticket to the prize giving, nor was he invited to the house where all the Chinese were celebrating. He went to the other sailors' overnight party which I missed. Early the next morning, Jon and I managed to meet up on the top of Portland while the rest of the team were sleeping off the celebrations from the night before. We celebrated with champagne while watching a stunning sunrise. No words were needed at that fabulous and meaningful moment. We made it! Jon and Lily as a team, hand in hand, went through all the difficulties and barriers and achieved our ultimate goal – to be an Olympic Champion.

"Go confidently in the direction of your dreams. Live the life you've imagined." (Henry David Thoreau)

Chapter 2

My Family

I was born in 1987 in Shanghai, the largest city in China. Five of us shared a two bedroom flat which was just 20 square metres. My grandparents lived in one room, while I shared the other room with my parents, all sleeping on the same bed. This is how it was for the majority of city dwellers – only suburban families would have their own, more spacious, home.

My parents started dating shortly after they were introduced to each other by a friend. To me their relationship felt more or less like a business partnership – they never shared genuine love with each other. This is not uncommon in China where 'matching' is very important for couples: matching family background, education, appearance, property, savings and income. This may sound strange and superficial to western readers, but, with a history of arranged marriages for hundreds of years, the freedom to choose who to marry is already a significant step forward!

My mum, who stands at 174cm, was considered very tall in China, and this caused her a lot of problems in finding a partner. Dad turned up just in time, with a height of 180cm; Shanghainese; big eyes; smart mind; humorous and the youngest in his family, meaning he was well taken care of.

My father took advantage of the fact that he could stay in my mum's home with her parents because she was the only child in Shanghai (my mum's brothers and sisters lived in another province). He sees my mother as a tall, quiet and diligent woman who can do all the housework.

Their approach to choosing and deciding on a marriage partner was based on this belief in matching, and they don't see anything wrong with this since it is what happens for most Chinese. They do not believe there is true love in this world and are quite happy with the idea of finding a suitable match to make do with. I have never heard them saying "I love you", or kissing or hugging (at least not in front of me). It seems that all their love was directed towards me.

However, at the same time, I also experienced many quarrels and domestic violence. My father has a bad temper and he can fight with anyone when he loses it. As a result, both my grandma and my mum suffered physically and mentally, but they never called the police, just the ambulance.

I once asked my mother how she could put up with this and whether she had ever thought about divorce. Without doubt she experienced a lot of pain and had considered separation, but she was never brave enough to take any action, fearing the effect it would have on me and the family's reputation.

I once said to her: "Mum, if you are not happy in your life with dad, you should divorce and find another path which may give you joy. Do not let how it looks to others hinder your pursuit of a healthy, enjoyable and meaningful life." But she refused, however hard I tried to persuade her.

I love my parents, but I must admit that I don't relish staying with them for a long period as the atmosphere is often negative; filled with lots of complaints, criticism, blame and argument.

Their approach to parenting was again rather different to what most readers would be used to. My dad would usually punish me if I made a mistake. I would be made to kneel on a wooden washboard and he would slap my face or smack my bottom with slippers. The most serious punishment was when they shut me outside and did not allow me back into the flat.

All of these things happened before I was 10 years old, because it was then that I left home to sail, and it never happened afterwards because I had so little holiday to go back home and see my parents.

I didn't feel particularly bad about these punishments at the time because the same things happened to many other children. But, looking back on it, I think it was probably one of the reasons why my character is to be obedient and why I behave as a 'good girl' (as perceived by Chinese parents). However, in the long term I do think it had some negative effect; stopping me thinking critically for myself.

My parents also taught me to be a mean, stingy person – to keep things for myself rather than share with others. This is a Shanghai trait. The Shanghainese have a good reputation for being shrewd and smart, but a bad one for being selfish and hostile. They have an enormous sense of pride in being from a big city and see themselves as superior to others. For example, many parents from Shanghai would forbid their children to marry a person from another province. What is more, those living in Shanghai city would even be against the idea of finding a partner from rural places within the Shanghai province.

Shanghai citizens used to regard outsiders as poor, dirty and uncivilised, and this idea is deeply rooted in my parents' generation. I would guess this is declining as my generation tend to be more open, tolerant and well educated.

I am pleased that, once I started sailing, the team life helped me to cultivate a more generous and cooperative personality. After travelling around China, I have found people in other provinces to be more friendly, warm-hearted and enthusiastic.

*

I didn't learn about healthy eating from my parents as they encouraged me to eat a lot of food, which they thought was good for me. For example, five eggs, dozens of chicken legs or wings, a big bowlful of shrimps, animal organs or pigs' feet might all be eaten in one meal, along with drinking 2,000ml of milk and 1,000ml of yoghurt every day. Mostly they deep fried the food to make it taste delicious, then stir- or pan-fried using lots of pork oil, salt or soy sauce.

It wasn't until later on, when I needed to lose weight for the Optimist dinghy, that I started to try vegetables and fruit.

Now, after years as a professional sportswoman, and having read some books on nutrition, my diet is much healthier. But when I try to convince my parents of the benefit of a balanced diet and eating nutritious foods, they still refuse to change or accept what I say. They say that the Chinese have had no problems eating the way they have done for thousands of years.

*

I cannot leave talking about my parents without mentioning some things that I inherited from them. I was born partially deaf, with about half the hearing of an ordinary person – this was inherited from my father who had about two thirds of his hearing. My left eye can barely make out anything due to poor sight, called amblyopia, which was passed on from my mother.

I have since discovered that both of these disabilities can be corrected or improved, if found out early and treated before the age of 12. It was a pity that my parents did not take these hereditary problems seriously and missed the opportunity to solve and fix them. They obviously have a huge impact on my daily life.

Nevertheless I appreciate my parents so much for giving me life, providing me love and raising me to the best of their ability.

*

China is progressing so rapidly and its people are advancing generation by generation: my grandmother was illiterate, unable to read or write; my mother only did the compulsory education in primary and middle school; I finally had the chance to study at university. The Chinese will become more international, more open and more enlightened with globalisation. But we should always be aware of what has happened in the past, and remember our history to learn from it, while marching boldly into a new era.

Interlude 1: A Balanced Life

I cannot over-emphasise the importance of balance in our daily life. We need to ensure that there is a balance between:

- Training and rest
- Study and fun
- Eating healthy food and the food you enjoy (maybe some junk food)

I firmly believe that it is only when you are getting a high level of satisfaction and enjoyment from both your family (and friends) and your career (work, study or sport) that you can truly be happy and successful.

I felt it was a pity that there were so many strict team regulations which meant that I, like other Chinese athletes, was not able to see my family and spend time with them. I only saw them once or twice a year for one or two weeks' holiday.

Family and friends play a crucial role in giving us the emotional strength and extra motivation and support that are needed on our journey to conquer all the difficulties and challenges that we face as professional athletes.

I was envious of all the other foreign sailors who could go home every so often, or after some regattas. I also wanted to socialise with friends outside the team, with foreign sailors in pubs or parties. But my communication with them was very limited, through the internet or letters.

We should be grateful to our parents who give us life; to

our friends for their company and support; to our mentors, teachers, coaches and leaders who guide us in the right direction with powerful knowledge; and for all the things that we have and the beauty that is around us – it is a blessing to live in this wonderful world.

Chapter 3

Becoming a Sportswoman

I was like a tomboy in my early years: short haircut, loud voice, playing with boys, hyperactive, loving adventures and trying new things, doing everything fast, and so on. Because of this non-girly character, my parents decided to let me try some sports in the hope that I would be quieter after some intensive training.

On seeing a poster for a district swimming team outside my pre-school front gate, they sent me to see a swimming coach, which was followed by some test exercises. Luckily I was accepted by the Changning District Swimming Team of Shanghai. So my sports career started at the age of 5.

The swimming pool was quite far away from my home, and my parents spent two hours every day taking me to and fro and waiting outside the swimming pool to pick me up. Like most parents they brought me some snacks or fruit as a reward after hard training. The training schedule was two hours swimming every day after school and at weekends. There was only one day off a year: Chinese New Year.

My best stroke was freestyle and I was particularly good at endurance. Each year, in June, there was a big competition with other district teams and I got many medals in long distance freestyle and team relays.

This was pretty much my life for the next five years: my whole time was devoted to study and swimming.

From childhood, I was a hard worker and I would do fitness training by myself during the school holidays. There was a popular Japanese TV series at the time called 'The Flame of Youth'. It told the story of a female volleyball player and her campaign for the Olympics. I found it very inspiring as she conquered numerous setbacks and difficulties, and she trained extremely hard all the time. I even learnt some exercises from her, like frog jumps, handstands, running uphill and so on. It was at that time that a little seed of an Olympic dream was planted inside my heart.

In 1996, when the Olympics were held in Atlanta, USA, I watched some of the sports on television with admiration and envy. My father teased me by saying "Will I see you on TV one day, representing China in the Olympic Games?" I smiled silently as it was all so far away for me at the time – I wasn't even in the Shanghai Swimming Team, so how could I realistically aim for the top podium in the world? But, even so, his little tease fired up my motivation even more and I was determined to do my best and do it well, every single day, to realise my big dream.

At this stage, my family was unaware that the whole pattern of their life would soon change dramatically.

One day, while my parents were waiting outside the swimming pool, a lady approached them, talking about the sport of sailing and asked about my year of birth. She was the Shanghai Optimist Sailing Coach, Juliet, who was trying to find some new sailors for the team born in either 1986 or 1987 (aged around 10).

(The reason for the interest in a specific age was because

Chinese Optimist sailors are primarily trained to prepare for the National and Asian Games which are held every four years. So, for each four year cycle, they aim to have the most mature sailors peaking at those Games, before they reach the Optimist class's age limit. This means that there is always a three or four year gap between Chinese Optimist sailors.)

Juliet scanned me up and down carefully and then asked me if I would like to try sailing. "What is that?" I asked. "It's steering a boat on the water." she explained, "Why not give it a try; you may well love it and not want to get off the boat afterwards." As sailing was very rare in China, the first thing that popped into my dad's mind was a windsurfer jumping, turning and surfing in big waves.

Juliet left her contact details and said that there would be a two week selection camp the following week and encouraged my parents to give me the chance to experience a whole new sport. Later mum and dad asked me whether I would like to give it a try and I happily agreed. Trying new things has always been one of my favourite activities!

On 27th June 1997, dad drove me for two hours to the Shanghai Water Sports Centre which is located in a suburb right by Dianshan Lake. It was the first time that I had ever been to such a remote place outside the city, with lots of green areas, a standard rowing lake and spacious open water.

It was also the first time for Lily to leave home and stay overnight in another place without her parents. I was assigned to share a room with five other pupils. It was very exciting to live together with several children the same age as me. But the strange thing was that I couldn't understand their accent very well, which caused a lot of misunderstanding. It reminds me of one of the English texts I'd learnt in school: "The English understand each other, but I don't understand them. Do the English speak English?" And now this happened to me – we were all Shanghainese but, as a city dweller, I didn't understand the rural residents!

Everything was so new to me: team life; washing my clothes; eating in a huge dining hall with other professional sportspeople (rowers, kayakers, windsurfers and water-skiers); training in a gym; and the most exciting of all – sailing in an Optimist!

After some demonstrations on land, I was then taken out in the boat by a 'master' Optimist sailor who was four years older than me (in the four year cycle ahead of me). She taught me patiently while steering the boat and then let me sail myself. About two hours later, she moved into a RIB and I started to sail alone. It didn't start well – the moment she left, everything became a mess. I capsized several times and my head was hit by the boom when gybing. Thanks to the buoyancy aid and my swimming skills, I was able to get back into the boat again quickly once it was righted. Despite those embarrassments, nothing alarming happened and I was having a lot of fun playing on and off the water.

During the two weeks, more than fifty students from all over Shanghai were assessed through a series of exercises and drills including sailing, fitness, flexibility, reactivity, intelligence and enthusiasm. In the end only three girls were accepted, and I was one of the lucky few.

However, the day I was picked up by my parents after finishing the training camp, the three of us and two of my swimming coaches had a sleepless night. We met together immediately to discuss the new situation. Obviously the swimming coaches wanted to keep me in the swimming team and argued that swimming was a much more popular sport whereas hardly anybody knew about sailing at the time. There were millions of professional swimmers, table tennis players and divers in China, but less than five hundred sailors in total!

Meanwhile my parents tried to evaluate the pros and cons of being a sailor. Mum didn't want me to switch because taking up sailing would mean that I would be away from home most of the time as training would be held outside Shanghai, making it impossible to have much family time together. Dad, on the other hand, was quite supportive of choosing sailing because he saw it as a completely new realm to explore. It would be good for my personal development and I would learn many independent skills living with a team and not relying on my parents for everything all the time.

In the end, although my parents appeared very reluctant to let me accept the offer, they still gave me the right to make the final decision. Even though I was only 10 years old at the time, I realised that this would be a life changing decision. I said to them that I thought sailing was much more interesting than swimming and, for me, swimming back and forth in the pool every day was a bit dull – just like doing chores. In sailing, however, no two single days or races would be exactly the same. There would be lots going on, requiring me to think, observe and interact with other boats. In addition, I enjoyed the freedom of moving in the open water, the closeness to nature and the fresh air. I said I was deeply fascinated by sailing and wanted to explore the world with wind and water. So I chose the sport of sailing.

The freedom was particularly appealing because I felt my life was limited by my poor hearing and eyesight. Young children laughed at me, made fun of me, and didn't allow me to join their activities due to my lack of these basic human functions. So the moment I boarded a boat, a deep sense of freedom suddenly overwhelmed my body, heart and mind. I loved to be in the boat surrounded by nature which isn't judgemental; just fresh, open and vast! I had never been so happy and fulfilled as I was on a boat.

Both my parents and swimming coaches respected my decision. My father said, "Lily, this is the road you chose yourself. So whenever or whatever hardship confronts you, you must keep marching bravely ahead and never give up!" My mother cried for several nights on end as she couldn't accept that I would be leaving home for a long time. I had been her life from when she was pregnant, through giving birth to me and over the ten years she brought me up, and all of a sudden she could no longer be with me.

In contrast to her, I was completely positive about being a sailor – totally ignorant of what challenges and tough situations lay ahead of me. It was my choice and I would never regret it.

From then on a journey full of self-discovery and exploration started, opening the first page of Lily's sailing world.

Positive Affirmation 1: 100% Concentration

I completely focus on what I am doing. The true joy comes from being fully present in each and every moment. Things are more likely to go my way when I don't worry about anything (whether I am going to win or lose), but focus my full attention on what's happening right at this moment. I enjoy doing something I choose and plan to do, and fully concentrate on it at that time.

I don't care about what other people might think of me as long as I am doing the right thing for myself. What others are doing or eating doesn't matter to me and I stick to my own schedule. I control what I do and perform the best I can. I think only about what I am doing and don't allow anything else to bother or distract me.

I talk to myself to remind and encourage me to devote my mind wholly to what I am doing and doing it well. Whenever I do a good job, I say: "That's me, well done!" If I am diverted, I say "It's none of my business, ignore it, switch it off" to help me refocus and get back on track.

I remain in the here and now. Wherever I am, I am all there. I focus completely on what I do.

Chapter 4

Training to be a Professional

For the first two months, while training in Shanghai, every morning we studied together in a new primary school near the Water Sports Centre. Then in the afternoon we sailed and did physical training, finishing off with homework in the evening.

During that time my parents would visit me once every two weeks and brought me lots of snacks. They were very pleased to see how much I had learnt and improved: I could wash clothes and dishes myself, make the bed and clean the room and I was getting on well with teammates and coaches alike. At the same time, they felt sad because my hands had become rough and my skin turned brown having been exposed to the sun for a long time while sailing and doing heavy training.

Most Chinese children are too pampered and protected by their parents or grandparents and they do not do any housework. It is not until a teenager goes to study at university that they start to learn how to live independently. Also white skin colour is what Chinese desire the most. They are so afraid of the sun that in the summer many people use umbrellas to shade themselves from the sunlight, or wear long trousers and sleeves, even when the temperature is up to 35 degrees.

Once the winter comes, Shanghai is a bit too cold for sailing.

All the provincial sailing teams would move to southern cities or towns (such as Fujian, Guangdong and Hainan province) for winter training. So in October 1997 I travelled with the team for three days by train, bus and ferry to Haikou – on Hainan Island just opposite the mainland (Sanya is also on this island).

From then on I only went back home and saw my parents once or twice a year for a few days' holiday after a major national championship. Because Shanghai has no suitable sea to sail on, I was travelling all year round, with winter in the south of China and summer in the north (in places like Qingdao in Shandong province or Dalian in Liaoning province).

What about education? The school would send a different teacher to the team each month to rotate and the study time was reduced to every evening, Sunday (our rest day) or when the weather was too bad to sail.

So I became a full-time sailor not long after my 10th birthday.

As the technology wasn't as advanced as it is today, one of my routines for the first few years was to make a phone call to my parents and write them a letter every week. I shared with them what I had learnt, how I was progressing in both sailing and study, coaches' comments and feedback, and interesting stories about teammates. I would not talk about negative things to prevent them from worrying about me.

In reality, the training at Haikou was much more intensive than it had been in Shanghai. A typical training day started at 6am with an early morning aerobic session. After breakfast the coaches would decide whether to sail in the morning or afternoon and then set another strength fitness session based on the sailing time. I broke equipment and injured myself and some people made fun of me because of my hearing problems.

During the first month I missed home terribly and couldn't help crying every time I opened a new letter from my family. Once I received a letter while having lunch. All of a sudden I burst into tears and everyone thought that a tragedy had happened at home. Juliet came and asked me what was wrong, and I replied "nothing", but couldn't stop crying. She took the letter, read the contents and came to realise that nothing special had happened – I was just homesick. I missed my parents' love, care and company so much, but our next meeting was so far away and so brief. It is really sad that, all too often, we only realise the preciousness of people or the value of things when we lose them.

I didn't get on very well with most of the boys in the team because they often joked about my disabilities and refused to let me join their activities. Even with some other people in the team, I could feel their impatience and unwillingness to repeat words when I missed something or said "pardon". Sometimes, when I failed to hear what the coaches said, I just watched what the other sailors were doing and tried to follow them. Other times I felt so guilty about asking people to repeat themselves that I pretended I understood and then did something completely wrong. The Chinese made no effort to conceal their amusement and laughed loudly in front of me, complaining how hard it was to make things clear to me.

As a result, I felt lonely, remote and alienated. Gradually I became quieter and quieter and just kept things to myself, which affected my confidence and self-esteem even more. Nevertheless, I wouldn't let these things knock me down easily: I was going to prove myself and show that I could achieve a successful sports career through hard work and learning, despite my physical frailties.

Some of my teammates did not set a good example of self-discipline in training. If a coach was around, they would follow the plan and do it well. But once the coach had left for some reason, they would relax and chat, while pretending to do some movements. Discussing how to ask for sick leave was also a popular subject: some would pretend to be ill; others would claim to have a pain here or there. However, the coaches were very aware of the tricks they were playing, which led to distrust between the parties. They were therefore very strict with the sailors, not approving a day off from training when people felt unwell. There were occasions when I had to go out sailing in cold, wet days even when I had a fever, cough, flu, stomach ache or badly infected skin which left me with many deep scars for the rest of my life.

I don't know why I am different in this respect, but I have never needed to be pushed to train hard. I know that I am doing the training for myself, not for the coaches or leaders, or to show off or play games with other people. I wonder if I was just born a hard worker, as I am eager to learn and never stop trying to improve myself, both on and off the training scene.

In my spare time I would do some self-study and read lots of books, or reflect on my sailing while others watched the TV, played computer games or cards, or just gossiped. In some ways, the fact that I cannot hear properly helps me focus on the task in hand and I am rarely distracted by other things. I am also never woken up by heavy rain or thunder in the middle of the night, which helps me get good quality sleep.

Speaking of sleep, the bed I was allocated also improved with my growing body and status in the team. For the first year, two sailors shared a single bed. In the second year, three shared a double bed. From the third year onwards I finally got the privilege of sleeping alone in a single bed. Phew...

*

In the early years there were no marinas in China at all, so sailors had to launch off the beach or through soft mud, and deal with big waves that only surfers would want. It was not until preparing to host the 2008 Beijing Olympic Games that numerous world-class marinas emerged along the Chinese coastline.

Back in those days, launching was the most miserable memory I had in sailing: I broke so much equipment (like masts, booms, sails and spars) and injured myself on my head, face, legs and back – almost everywhere on my body. Once I was buried underneath a huge wave and the power of nature was so strong that I couldn't swim to the surface for about a minute, drinking lots of salty water. When I was finally washed ashore, I lay exhausted on the beach watching the sky, glad to still be alive!

Team spirit played a huge role as the Europe and Laser sailors would help by sending the Optimists out first. The young sailors would get in their Optimist, fit the rudder on and get the daggerboard ready, while the bigger sailors would swim out into the sea, holding the bow to keep it facing the breaking waves, until past them and it was safe to let the Optimist sailor steer out themselves. Subsequently the Laser boys would do the same for the female Europe sailors before they launched themselves. The design of the Laser had the advantage that, even when the cockpit was full of water, it could still move forwards, whereas the Optimist and Europe have much bigger cockpits and once this was full it was impossible to move through the water.

After the day's sailing session, the process was repeated. The boys would come back first, surfing the waves in with care. They then swam out to a point beyond the breaking waves. One or two of them would hold a Europe or Optimist, crashing back to shore following the breaking waves. Some were lucky, but not all, which was why we spent an awful lot of time repairing damaged equipment to allow us to sail again as quickly as possible.

On another occasion we were caught in a heavy storm, gusting up to 40 knots, with the waves rising to 5 metres high. Unfortunately the coach boat had capsized, flipped over by a gigantic wave, and was upside down. We were all in the middle of the sea, with no land or buildings in sight. The more experienced sailors slowed down to sail close together, as a big group, in case someone encountered a problem.

For the first time I cried on my sailboat as I've never felt so close to death. Humans are so insignificant when exposed to the force of nature. I prayed to god, hoping he would save us from this disaster. After three hours of bouncing up and down while slowly reaching to the shore we finally got to the closest beach before the daylight disappeared. Luckily none of the equipment on our boats was damaged that time (which was quite unusual) and the coaches were picked up by a local fishing boat not long after.

Though this horrible and unforgettable experience occurred when I was still less than 11 years old, it never stopped me chasing my dream as I believed the rainbow would always shine after a storm.

Positive Affirmation 2: Positive Thinking

I am a positive thinker and this contributes to an optimistic attitude. I am happy, healthy and have abundant love. I only speak about, see and reflect upon what I want. I can have, do, or be anything I want – no limits. I concentrate on what I wish to experience as energy goes where attention flows. I hold the key in my hand to every aspect of my life – the key to my thoughts and feelings. I know how incredibly powerful the spiritual side is. My mind is actually shaping the world around me.

Whenever I become negative, I stop and move myself off that wavelength and then shift to the positive channel by saying: "WARNING! CHANGE THINKING NOW!" I take a few moments and do several Rapid Eye Movements to completely let go of the bad feeling and replace it with loving, joyful ones.

The universe is friendly, supportive and brings all good things to me. I recognise the beautiful and wonderful things around me, and embrace, bless, praise them. I listen to my thoughts and listen to the words I am saying. I quieten my mind and use meditation as my daily practice. I go for the inner joy, inner peace and inner vision first. I am grateful for all the things that I feel. I give thanks for it, feel the joy of it and truly appreciate it.

I think perfect thoughts. I say to myself: I see only perfection; I am perfection! I am important, competent, talented, unique, brave, fantastic, smart, compassionate, strong, enthusiastic, powerful, whole, loving, harmonious, and happy all my life. I must tell myself: How brilliant I am!

Chapter 5

My Optimist Years

After one year of full-time training, I had the chance to do the Optimist National Championship in Hong Kong in 1998. Because of the four year cycle to fit with the National and Asian Games, all the experienced, older Chinese sailors had retired from the class due to the age limit being 15. So almost all the fleet were aged 11 or 12, like me, apart from some from Hong Kong and other international sailors who also came to do the event.

Shanghai had been dominating the Optimist Nationals for years and now it was my turn to defend it. I managed to win the championship quite easily as I only needed to beat my teammates and contemporaries from other provinces. We also defended the Team Racing title which entitled us to represent China at the next Asian and World Optimist Championship. (For the Optimist class in China, where there is no National Team Squad, the provincial team that wins the Nationals represents the country at International events).

One month later I did the Asia Championship, which happened to be held in Shanghai. This time the fleet was much stronger and there were many very good and experienced sailors from Japan, Korea, Singapore and Thailand. In the end I wasn't even in the top ten overall and was only third in the girls' fleet, which was far from fulfilling.

It was not until the World Championship, held in Martinique, France in 1999, that I had the first taste of the real competitiveness of the top world sailors. Wow – about 250 boats, with each start having more than 70! I was shocked to learn that sailing with so many boats meant that a little mistake could cost you dozens of places. The way the elite sailors controlled the fleet so well really impressed me. It made me realise how big the gap was between me and them and how much I needed to improve.

It is embarrassing to tell you that I wasn't even in the top 150 after 15 races and that China didn't qualify for the top 16 teams for the Team Racing. But, in spite of all that, I was very fortunate to be doing international events on behalf of the National Team at such an early age. I was still young and had plenty of time to keep improving and progressing in my sailing career.

In 2000, a new group of Optimist sailors joined the Shanghai Team and each of the 'old' sailors was responsible for teaching a new sailor (just as I had been taught). This is an interesting team tradition as, once the relationship develops, we call each other 'master' and 'apprentice' for the rest of our lives.

Three years ago, when I was an apprentice, we were assigned to different masters, but this new generation had the chance to choose their own masters. When the coach said "start", all the girls were running towards me, as they thought I was the best female sailor in the team. Echo, a girl from the suburb of Nanhui District, was the first to reach me and so she won the 'game' of choosing the master she wanted the most. The rest of the girls had to turn to my other female teammates.

Once the pairs were set, the competition began: the results

of each day's sailing of the paired masters and apprentices were added together as a team and contributed to weekly and monthly overall standings.

I gave all I had and shared everything with Echo, who seemed to be progressing pretty fast. Each training day I would spend hours briefing and debriefing her: talking to her about this, teaching her about that, demonstrating how to do it and giving her top tips. I often finished the day with a sore throat and not able to speak another word.

Obviously not all the masters would give their utmost and so many other apprentices joined me when I was teaching Echo. The other young sailors were envious of Echo for having a 'teacher' who was not only good at sailing herself, but also enthusiastic, patient and kind to her 'student'.

Echo later dominated in the Optimist once my generation left the class. When she retired from the Optimist, she quickly adapted to the Olympic Laser Radial class and became a very competitive racer in light wind. She pushed me hard while I was campaigning for both the Beijing and London Olympic Games and our relationship remains good. We could be hard with each other on the water, such as match racing each other, while taking great care of each other off the water as we always shared the same room in the National or Shanghai Sailing Team.

She is a huge fan of music but, whenever she saw me studying, reading or just wanting to have a quiet time, she would immediately turn down the volume or use headphones. She has also been so considerate, helping me to carry stuff when I was suffering from lower back pain. Nowadays we no longer call each other 'master' and 'apprentice' as we used to, but 'Xu' and 'Shuang' which is one character of our real Chinese names. I am sure our friendship will last forever and I send her my very best wishes for her campaign for the Rio Olympics in 2016. It is your time to show the world Echo – play hard and enjoy!

In my final two years in the Optimist dinghy, I won all the girls' titles in the National, Asia and World Championship as well as the National and Asian Games which are held once every four years.

I first became a World Champion in Qingdao, China in 2001. In theory I should be pretty proud of that, but I am not. Most foreign sailors were not familiar with a venue where the current was sometimes faster than the Optimist's boat speed. I had learnt how to deal with this through sculling (propelling the boat illegally by frequently adjusting the rudder) while making sure that the Judges did not see. This worked pretty well, although I was protested for it by a group of sailors and was disqualified from one race.

What I struggle to understand now is why I didn't feel bad or guilty about this action which not only broke the rules, but also severely infringed the principles of sportsmanship and fair play. I find this very difficult to accept now and feel ashamed while writing it down. But I want to be 100% honest and a moral person for the rest of my life. I am very concerned about any negative influence on young Chinese sailors and I want to help them get rid of these terrible habits through proper guidance and good education.

During the event, on 13th July, the IOC President Samaranch announced that Beijing had won the bid for hosting the 2008 Olympic Games. Huge crowds gathered together in the city centre of Qingdao celebrating the victory as the sailing competition would be held there in seven years' time. From then on, competing in the Olympics in my home country became my highest goal.

The following year, I defended my World Championship title in Texas, USA in 2002. This time I was very happy as I won through superior sailing and I received warm, genuine congratulations from people everywhere. Months later I finished my fantastic Optimist career by becoming the Asian Games Champion in Busan, Korea. That was a really awesome experience: living in the Athletes' Village with different sportspeople; the impressive Opening and Closing Ceremonies in an immense stadium; the 24-hour international dining hall; and the huge media coverage. I was exposed to so many fun experiences for the first time!

*

What sounds like a perfect youth sailing career was actually accompanied by many sacrifices. The most significant one was missing my menstrual cycle for two years due to losing weight. While my height rose to 174cm, I had to keep my weight under 50kg to be at the optimum for the small Optimist dinghy. Those years were right in the middle of puberty and my body was deprived of nutrients to grow normally. Every day I could only have an egg and a carton of milk for breakfast, soup and vegetables for lunch and fruit for dinner.

Juliet would weigh us every evening and sailors had to go out running for an hour if they were over the target weight. There were times when I fainted or suddenly lost consciousness if I stood up too quickly from sitting or lying. Other times I couldn't concentrate at all, making mistakes here and there. For this reason my body fat was too low to produce enough female hormones needed for menstruation. If I could go back in time, I wouldn't allow myself to do this again, having learnt how damaging it is to one's health. But this is still the practice in China – nothing matters apart from getting good results.

Another restriction imposed on us in the Shanghai Optimist Team was that we weren't allowed to be feminine: to have long hair, wear dresses or low collar sleeveless tops. Perhaps the coaches didn't want the girls to waste any time on dressing to be prettier, but preferred them to spend all their time training and sailing. Or maybe they wanted to minimise gender differences to avoid affairs in the team. Or they simply wanted to control everything, even if it was unrelated to the sport.

However, as a result, I was very much like a tomboy, because I was so sun-tanned, with a very short boy-style haircut. This led to many embarrassing experiences when I went to the toilet. Some would scream at seeing a 'boy' come into the women's lavatory; others would direct me to the men's washroom.

On another occasion, some Optimist sailors only realised that I was a girl when I won the Asia Championship and stepped onto the girls' podium! I could see the bewilderment and shock on their faces, but I actually felt quite proud of myself, racing competitively against those boys, who didn't treat me differently because they were unaware that they were competing against a girl for the whole regatta! At other times I was called 'little boy', 'sir' or 'Mr'. Because of this, the moment I finished in the Optimist class I immediately started to grow my hair longer in the hope of getting rid of such comments and to become more girly.

That's pretty much it for my Optimist years. I changed so much both in outside appearance and inside, mentally. I grew from 130cm to 176cm in height and from 30kg to 60kg in weight. I picked up sailing and became an Optimist World Champion. I learnt how to be a better person by helping others, sharing with people and giving generously. I had the experience of travelling by train, plane and ferry, visiting many parts of China, and travelled overseas. It opened my eyes and broadened my horizons. All of this wouldn't have been possible without sailing, due to the restrictions of my family background and their financial position. How lucky I was!

I imagine that many readers from well-developed countries, where these things are more easily accessible, may well take them for granted. But please be grateful for what you have and the people around you. Life is so full of beauty so long as we truly open our eyes with a positive attitude and give genuine thanks for everything.

Interlude 2: Eat to Perform

I used to wonder why I trained so much but gained very little fitness. One of the huge mistakes I made was that I didn't eat carbohydrates. When I sailed an Optimist I had to lose weight, and since the Optimist was not that physically demanding, it was not too bad without carbohydrates. But once I switched to the bigger Olympic classes, such as the Europe and Laser Radial, there was no way I could hike (lean out) hard without enough energy stored in my body.

After reading some books on nutrition, I was shocked to realise how terrible my diet was to support the amount of training I was doing. I was a professional athlete who needed to deal with a high intensity workload every day. The popular low carb types of food in supermarkets were not suitable for me. Athletes need energy from carbohydrates to convert to sugar in order to feed their bodies with energy. Every meal or snack we choose must contain at least 50% of carbs. Sugar gives immediate but short energy, whereas complex carbohydrates have a much more stable yet longer function to continuously support your workout.

Eat little and often, 5-6 medium meals instead of 3 normal large ones. Choose complex carbohydrates rather than simple carbohydrates to get more fibre. Choose a rainbow of vegetables and fruits. Consume healthy fat from nuts, olive or flaxseed oil, avocado, etc. Avoid processed food as much as possible; the more natural the food the better.

The best recovery window is to eat within half an hour

of your workout. I would always prepare some food so that I could have it right after the gym or sailing. It would be perfect if you could have a protein shake or juice as a combined drink at the same time.

Chapter 6

My Time in the Europe Class

Only two weeks after I competed in my last Optimist event at the Asian Games, I went to Hainan for the National Championship of the Europe class, which was then the Olympic single-handed dinghy for women. There were less than two years until the Athens Olympic Games, so this would be the best opportunity for me to qualify for the National Team which was the first step towards my Olympic dream.

After three pre-regatta training days in the new dinghy, I started the Championship while still asking how to adjust the equipment properly, how to steer the boat effectively, how to tack facing backwards (the opposite to an Optimist) and how to sail at perfect angles downwind. Consequently my technique was terrible because of a lack of familiarity with the class, lack of speed and not being able to control the boat very well!

However, armed with my existing sailing skills of good starting and catching the wind shifts, I managed to finish among the top eight, which enabled me to join the National Sailing Team for the following winter training camp. I believed that, once I had spent some time in the new boat, I would master the new techniques and progress quickly to catch up with my fellow Europe sailors.

The selection trials would start in mid-2003 and I needed to be competitive enough by then to beat the other Chinese sailors in order to get the spot of representing China at the Athens Olympic Games in 2004.

Unfortunately life doesn't always go the way we plan. In November 2002 I was diagnosed with a tumour in my left thighbone. The good news was that, after some tests, it turned out to be benign. Nevertheless, I was advised by doctors to have an operation to remove the tumour as soon as possible, otherwise I might lose my leg, or even my life, if it later became an incurable cancer. Everyone agreed with the doctors' suggestion, except me. I couldn't accept the fact that I wouldn't be able to sail for half a year after the surgery, which meant that I would miss the Olympic trials for Athens. But I had no choice except to follow everyone else's wishes.

Since the tumour was growing inside the bone, the bone would be empty once they had cleared out the tumour, so a new bone was needed to replace it. The doctor who was going to perform the operation gave me some information about the size of bone needed and where to buy it. Then mum accompanied me to another hospital which sold bones donated anonymously by people who had died. I remember it cost around £500. Carrying the iced bone in my hand, imagining it would soon be in my thigh, was a rather strange feeling.

I had the operation in December 2002 and it was the most extremely painful experience that I have ever had in my life. The moment I was pushed out of the surgery after the operation I tried to console my parents who looked very worried about my situation: "I'm all right, it wasn't as scary as people said. You see, I can still smile!"

Nonetheless, six hours later, when the effect of the anaesthetic had gone, I was in dreadful pain. Time went so slowly that every second felt a year long. What was worse, though, was a high temperature that developed. Unable to fight the pain, or get to sleep, tears flowed down my face for hours and hours. I couldn't move, couldn't eat, only bottles and drips with injections...

When I finally left the hospital in a wheelchair a few days later, the next miserable period followed – rehabilitation. At first my left leg couldn't bend at all. I had to start pushing and doing lots of painful exercises to regain the function of my leg, or lose it forever.

Meanwhile I devoted the majority of my time to learning English. Mum said to me one morning that she heard me muttering English in my sleep – was I trying to recite the texts I was learning? Yes – I wanted to talk with foreign sailors, I wanted to understand sailing terms and the rules in English, I wanted to learn from English books as well as other resources. Language has, without doubt, been a great tool to help me to connect with the world outside of China in my career.

While I was recovering in Shanghai doing some study, treatment and fitness training, I missed sailing terribly. Sometimes I would ponder how boring my life was without sailing. It was like a life without vigour, a picture without colour, or a movie without sound. It was in those quiet days, reflecting on myself and the past, that I realised how deeply I loved the sport of sailing. My life just couldn't continue without it. When I steered the boat it is actually the boat which was pointing out a route for me, guiding me towards my dream goal and life values.

*

When I was back in the Europe dinghy again, I cherished every single session. I wanted to maximise the effectiveness of training and make the most of every precious day, while I was still able to sail. I eventually joined the National Team at the end of 2003. Although I had no chance to participate in the 2004 Olympic Games, I was keen to improve and aim for the 2008 Olympics. I was progressing rapidly, achieving a second and then a first in the National Championships of 2004 and 2005.

When it was announced that the Europe class was being replaced by the Laser Radial from the 2008 Beijing Games onwards, I had no idea what it would mean or how it would affect me. All Chinese Europe sailors had to carry on in the Europe dinghy for another year before switching to the Laser Radial because the National Games in 2005 would still be raced in the Europe class.

In my two short years sailing the Europe, I missed the World Championship in Cagliari, Italy in 2004 due to visa issues. By the time I attended the 2005 Worlds in Rizhao, China, the fleet was much smaller and less competitive than it used to be because it had been kicked out of the Olympic family and many professional sailors had already moved to the Radial class. The Chinese dominated the fleet, with only one foreign sailor in the top eight. I was told by my coaches and leaders to deliberately finish fourth instead of third, letting a foreign sailor take the last podium place. They felt that for China to win all three medals would be very embarrassing and they should avoid humiliating the foreign sailors. How absurd!

Before the National Games in September, the Chinese Sailing Federation decided to send me to the International Sailing Federation (ISAF) Youth World Championship in Busan, competing in the girls' Laser Radial class. I literally jumped into the new class for the first time in Korea for the practice race, asking my teammate (who was sailing the standard Laser in the boys' fleet) how to steer a Laser dinghy properly.

The Laser does not feel the same as the Europe, with a bigger rudder angle to steer, slower in light winds and more physically demanding. I used my strengths of great starting and perfect wind shift playing to compensate for my lack of boat speed. I was at a particular disadvantage tacking and downwind, because I had no idea how to roll the boat when tacking or sail by the lee downwind (in the Europe class we sailed on a broad reach).

Still I sailed competitively and nearly challenged Paige Railey from the USA who was the World Champion of the Laser Radial class. In the last race, I was leading by a long way when heavy fog descended and, all of a sudden, there were no other boats in sight. As I had no compass at that time, I thoroughly lost my direction. Later, I heard some whistles and saw a bunch of boats all heading towards the sound. The Race Officer had somehow made the decision to let the messy race continue. For this reason I lost my lead and the Championship and finished second overall, with Paige first and Alison Young from the UK finishing third.

*

Finally, in this chapter, I'd like to talk a little bit about the Chinese National Games, which is the biggest event for all Chinese athletes. In terms of importance it is just below the Olympic Games, even more important than the Asian Games.

It is a competition between the provinces and there are a lot of tricks played behind the scenes. I was very lucky to be selected to represent Shanghai each of the four times I competed in the National Games. The majority of sailors are exchanged to represent other provinces which don't have a sailing team. So, for example, the Shanghai Sailing Team has about 100 sailors in all the four single-handed classes. As only three sailors per province are allowed to compete in each class, the others are 'sold' to represent remote provinces like Yunnan, Xizang, Inner Mongolia and so on. Nevertheless, they were still expected to contribute to their mother province, helping Shanghai representatives to win gold in each class. That explains why the National Games is more or less like team racing in a fleet competition. So long as the team wins the title, everyone will be rewarded with considerable sums of prize money from the mother province.

Sounds ridiculous? Well, think how lucky you are in the west to compete in sports for yourself instead of someone else!

The battle between provinces starts well before the start of the National Games. The host team would not allow any opposing teams to use the newly built marina and facilities to store or launch their boats. As a result we had to find some other places nearby to be able to train at the racing venue and get familiar with the local conditions.

Once in Lianyungang, Jiangsu province, the Shanghai Sailing Team found some space to store all the boats and constructed a temporary slipway for launching. As we were in the midst of groups of fishing boats, we had to sail our boats out carefully through the narrow gaps between them. On some occasions, when we were unable to avoid the low spring tide, we had to walk through the shallow water with soft mud up to our knees, step-by-step, while pulling the boat by hand for hundreds of metres. We then had to spend another hour washing the mud off the boats after coming ashore!

But things like this did not knock us down that easily. The teamwork and spirit played a huge role in helping everyone deal positively with the adversity. Any negative emotions melted away the moment the Shanghai sailors claimed all the championship titles in the single-handed dinghy classes. In the end, were those little tricks played by the host really worthwhile? Shouldn't we build a more friendly relationship and create a healthy competitiveness so that all Chinese sailors can work, develop and progress together?

Positive Affirmation 3: My Team and Teammates

I am honoured to be in the Shanghai and National Sailing Team. I enjoy the atmosphere which is full of energy and vitality. I love being with my teammates, coaches, leaders, assistants, and all the team members. We are tied together and help each other to reach our committed goal – the National Games, World Championships and Olympic Gold Medals!

Team always comes first rather than the individual, and since giving is a powerful action, giving with a generous heart feels even better and is one of the most joyous things I can do. I train hard and sail smart to keep improving and achieve my peak.

I focus only on what I appreciate about the others and think about all the reasons why I love them. I give the others the opportunity to create my happiness. I meditate every day and am grateful for all that I have. I read this affirmation frequently and grab every chance to meditate.

I love everything I own and I give all my love to everyone I know. I am overwhelmed by love.

Chapter 7

Studying English

Though there were very few opportunities to study while in the team, both my parents and coaches emphasised the importance of the English language and encouraged me to learn it. Some coaches even promised to send me abroad to train and race with top foreign sailors if my English was good enough – although that never happened!

What really drove my determination to learn English was the frustration of not being able to communicate with foreign sailors and the disadvantage of being unable to understand the documents and information related to racing. I simply couldn't accept these limitations due to not understanding English.

I utilised every spare minute in self-study before and after training. On a typical two- or three-session training day, I could squeeze in 2-4 hours of study and, if some sailing sessions were cancelled due to bad weather, or on rest days, the total time I spent studying increased. At first I needed to apply some self-discipline to resist the temptation of the entertainment that all my teammates were enjoying in the evening: playing cards, watching television, chatting, gossiping or shopping. But soon it became my natural habit and routine, so I no longer needed to force myself into the repetitive, dull learning exercises. Gradually it became a bonus as I started to enjoy the study process and was happy when I managed to understand more English and could talk to foreigners.

The classic English textbooks I used were the most popular ones in China in my generation (although they are now old and out of fashion): *New Concept English*. The whole series contains four books, with hundreds of texts. I applied a learning method from a professor which proved very effective:

- Learn new words
- Write down the text while listening to the tape
- Check the text and correct any mistakes
- Repeat the tape and read the text dozens of times to mimic the pronunciation
- Do the drills and learn the grammar
- Recite the text and then write it down in English and translate it into Chinese

This approach helped develop my all round English language skills, from listening and speaking, to reading and writing. During those days my throat was always sore as I had to read the texts over and over again to be able to follow the native pronunciation.

Meanwhile I used the Rule Book to learn sailing related terminology since there are many different meanings to ordinary English. For instance: running means downwind; reaching means crosswind; boom is a spar connected to the mast; and so on. I also used English movies or TV series to 'kill two birds with one stone': entertaining myself, but still learning English at the same time. Among my favourites were *Friends*, *Lost* and *Prison Break*.

After a few years, I started to act as a translator and all my teammates would turn to me whenever they needed some language help. Whenever there was a protest hearing, they would always prefer me to join them rather than the official team interpreter. The qualified interpreters knew very little about sailing and were not able to understand the sailor's situation well enough. For me those were golden opportunities both to practise my English and to improve my rules knowledge. It was just a bit strange that I became a frequent visitor to the protest rooms – I hope the International Judges didn't get bored seeing me so often!

Chapter 8

Learning from Others

After the National Games in 2005, my involvement with the Europe class came to an end. It was now the era of the Laser Radial class – the new women's Olympic single-handed dinghy from 2008 onwards. The top eight sailors from each class were selected for the National Sailing Team based on the results at the National Games.

But before we hit the start of the winter training camp, there was one important task – the army training. It was a two-week camp with army officers training us like soldiers. What was the idea behind athletes doing this? Well, the strict rules and discipline, obeying every command, acting or responding in exactly the same way, coping with severe conditions and difficulties, cultivating political morality and creating a spirit of patriotism are all 'virtues' the Chinese coaches and leaders would like us athletes to acquire.

There were also many positive changes as a result of the camp: team spirit and team work, enthusiasm to help each other, being brave in the face of adversity, an ability to execute well, improved fitness, an optimistic attitude, enhanced communication, understanding of organisations and management, and so on.

All sports teams in China have army training camps, but so do the majority of schools and universities at the beginning of a new year. "Once you are in the army training, you must comply with every instruction and have no right to say a single 'no'." This is a typical motto for soldiers which reflects exactly how the senior leaders want those of lower status to behave and how much they want to keep everybody tightly controlled.

Every day we got up early in the morning and started running while yelling numbers together in time. Before each meal we sang different army songs to show our loyalty and gratitude to the country as well as the Communist Party. There were another two sessions during the day when we would practise marching like soldiers, posture and positioning. The same thing was re-peated thousands of times until perfection was reached.

The most challenging one was standing still for hours and hours – and any little movement an officer spotted would cost us another 30 minutes' penalty. On one occasion my eyes suddenly turned all dark, I lost consciousness and fell to the ground. When I regained my feelings several minutes later, I felt a sharp pain on my head which I had bumped hard against a wall after losing control of my body.

Army life is not just about training, but also developing per-sonal discipline and habit. The room must be kept in an orderly way: the bed linen must be made up with exactly the right angle and size; with a precise place for shoes, hats, towels, cups, bowls and everything else. Each room was checked on a regular basis and anyone who broke these rules would be seriously penalised.

At the end of the camp, a performance examination, with military parade, took place. Top officers and leaders came to review the troops and mark them accordingly. A never-changing conversation takes place:

Officer:	"Hello, comrade!"
Comrade:	"Hello, officer!"
Officer:	"You have all worked very hard."
Comrade:	"We are here to serve the people of this country!"

The team that shouts the loudest, and is the neatest, will get the highest mark. The posture, marching, off-field behaviour, room cleanliness, and so on, determined the best team and the best individual person. The final result doesn't really matter very much, more important is the process by which we learnt how to apply the rigid army lifestyle and developed an unwavering determination to meet future challenges.

However, I feel that we should not lose our own personal interests, imagination and freedom by obeying everything demanded or threatened by senior people. The sad truth is that most Chinese are closely controlled and never bother to fight in the pursuit of a meaningful, loving and happy life.

Finally, in December 2005, we Chinese started our sailing campaign in the Laser Radial – one year after the rest of the world following the decision to change the women's Olympic single-hander at the 2004 ISAF Annual Conference. Due to some visa issues, I missed the 2005 World Championship in Brazil where Paige Railey was crowned World Champion.

I headed to Australia in January 2006 for the Sail Melbourne regatta after two weeks of training in the Laser. I was yet to feel familiar with the new boat, and my coach knew little about the Laser dinghy since he had never sailed one. I therefore had no idea how to adjust the equipment, trim the sail, of the fitness needed or the steering approach. All I could do was to observe how the other top sailors sailed the Radial which was totally new to me.

A hard lesson learnt from that regatta was that the kicking strap (vang) needs to be super tight while sailing upwind in light air – completely the opposite to the Europe where the kicker is always eased upwind. Another lesson was that Lasers normally sail by the lee (with the flow over the sail reversed) when going downwind, whereas a Europe is faster sailing on a broad reach.

This 'learning by looking' method meant that it took me much longer to master the new boat and I had to work out the reasons, or theories, behind everything all by myself. I was just so frustrated that I couldn't match the speed of the rest of the fleet, immediately reducing my chances of winning, irrespective of how well I did at the start or if I made the right decisions on the favoured side of the course. If the basic settings weren't right, then you had lost before you had even started.

I was desperate to find some resources (be they materials or people) to help me learn the proper way of sailing a Laser more efficiently, instead of exploring, testing and finding out myself. If the knowledge is already there and well communicated or handed down in some parts of the world, why was it necessary to waste time and take the wrong route over and over again?

But, even in those days, when I was so eager to find something or somebody to help me improve my Laser performance more quickly, I still didn't realise how limited the resources we had in China were compared to the majority of western countries. At that point, my knowledge of the English language was a useful tool to acquire information and knowledge from developed nations, especially those with a rich sailing heritage, like the UK and USA.

I started to search out some Laser and other sailing related publications in English, and used up almost all my salary buying them – an English book costs ten or twenty times more than a similar sized Chinese book! Despite the fact that it was an expensive investment, I couldn't have been more satisfied and delighted from reading, learning and improving with every single book.

Sail Fitter, by Michael Blackburn, an Australian Laser sailor and coach, who studied sports science for his doctoral degree, teaches readers how to do fitness training tailored specifically for sailing and windsurfing. I was grateful to him for his patient answers to my frequent e-mails full of questions. Later I designed and planned my own physical training following that book as well as Michael's personal guidance.

Before this, it was the Chinese sailing coaches who got sailors doing the simple basic fitness exercises such as running, pull ups, chin ups and squats. Even though the National Team would occasionally employ specialist physical trainers, it was hard for them to deliver the ideal programme since none of them knew anything about sailing.

For me it was very much a journey of self-exploration and self-discovery, seeking what might be helpful and useful to improve my sailing on my own until I had the honour of being coached by several foreign coaches.

*

In my 16-year dinghy career, I was coached by six foreigners.

The first one was Soren Johnsen from Denmark, multiple

World Champion in the men's Europe class. He joined the Shanghai Sailing Team in 2001 to help us campaign for the National Games that year in Shanwei, Guangdong province. Soren was the first ever foreign coach to enter the Chinese sailing arena, but since then many other coaches, from various parts of the world, have been invited to work with different provincial teams as well as the National Sailing Team.

I was only 14 years old, and sailing an Optimist, when Soren joined the team. He came mainly to help the Europe dinghy sailors with the aim of winning the National Games. However, since the whole team always trained together, he kindly offered to coach us all – a total of nearly fifty sailors from the Optimist, Europe and Laser classes.

He truly opened our eyes and widened our experience by bringing so many new things to the team. It was almost a revolutionary change which got rid of some of the stereotypical thinking among not only sailors from Shanghai, but also the whole of Chinese sailing. Many of those who benefitted from his coaching went on to the National Team squad and almost dominated in all three single-handed dinghies in the country.

A typical day kicked off at 6am with physical training. This was a nightmare for us at that time, not because we had to get up early, but because of the intensity of the training. This session lasted roughly two hours, combining both aerobics and strength. Since there were so many of us training together, there was no way to do it in a gym. So Soren took us running (sprinting on the beach and jogging) and climbing mountains for the first hour, followed by some body-weight or strength exercises to improve our general fitness for sailing.

The same routine happened every day, no matter whether

it was warm or cold, sunny or rainy. Initially the Chinese were shocked that Soren insisted on running outdoors when it was raining heavily, worried that the sailors would catch a cold or even a fever. However it turned out to be fine as we were kept active and were constantly out of breath, but, just to make sure, we took a shower immediately we finished.

Afterwards we would have breakfast at 8.30am, followed by a briefing for that particular day's sailing session which ran from 10am to 3pm. Since Soren had arrived we skipped the normal hot lunch and had a sandwich on the water instead to make the most of our sailing time. This was a big sacrifice for the Chinese, as we always have hot meals for lunch. Many sailors reported stomach aches or having no appetite while bobbing up and down in a boat. It took us some time to get used to this type of diet, but it actually cultivated a new way of eating which prepared us for future international regattas.

Straight after coming ashore, Soren would take us for a recovery session, including some jogging and stretching. This was another thing beyond the Chinese understanding as they believed that, after a windy day's sailing, jumping straight into bed for a sleep or nap would help the body recover quicker than doing light aerobics. But I definitely felt a huge difference after some active recovery exercise: to start with my body felt extremely tired, but half an hour later I was fresh and energetic again. Since then I kept this routine throughout my Olympic career – it is crucial so that you don't get up the following morning still feeling tired and sore.

After dinner our day finished with a long debrief as Soren would show us the videos he had taken, explain this and that, listen to the sailors' feedback, analyse the problems and discuss possible solutions. One of the words he emphasised the most was: 'THINKING!' This was an ability every Chinese sailor lacked: an inevitable consequence of their education, environment, society and culture.

Finally it was bed time and we could rest after a long, busy, hard working day. If you think we were relieved at the end of the day, then unfortunately you are wrong. We were thinking about what was waiting for us the next morning, hoping that time would stop and allow us to relax a bit longer. However, it was that hard training and huge effort that led the Shanghai Sailing Team to win two gold medals in the National Games in the Optimist and Europe classes – the best result my provincial team had ever achieved at that time.

The second foreign coach I worked with was Laurence Nicolas from France. She used to sail actively in the Europe dinghy and had coached many French sailors before moving to China where she served the National Sailing Team and two provincial teams from Jiangsu and Guangdon.

As a female coach she had the advantage of better communication and a closer relationship with the girls. In her time working with the National Team, Laurence helped the Chinese Europe sailors set many new records: achieving Olympic qualification in the first event, top ten in the World Championship and seventh in the Athens Olympics.

One of the Chinese leaders was very happy with the progress that Laurence had brought to the team, saying: "When I was watching on the water in the World Championship in the late 1990s, I had to count from the back of the fleet to see where the Chinese sailors were. Now, a few years later, the new generation has finished in the top eight at the Olympics and I can regularly see our sailors winning races. Counting from last is no longer the case for our Chinese sailors. What a remarkable advance!"

In addition to this, Laurence also helped two provincial teams make a tremendous improvement, frequently challenging the Shanghai team who had dominated for years and years. She now lives in Sanya, Hainan province, with her Chinese partner. Not surprisingly, she can now speak fluent Chinese and is still dedicating herself to promoting sailing in China.

Later, when I switched to the Laser Radial class I had two short term training arrangements with Ryan Eric Minth from the USA in 2006 and Karl Suneson from Sweden in 2007. Both of them taught me a lot about Laser-specific techniques, giving me a boost in boat speed in all wind conditions.

Before the 2009 National Games, Ashley Burning, from Australia, came to coach the Shanghai Sailing Team. This time Ash focussed mainly on the top three Laser men and Radial women sailors, instead of the whole team as Soren had done back in 2001. Ash really pushed the boys in fitness, helping them to conquer their strong wind weaknesses, which contributed to the first Laser National Champion for the Shanghai Sailing Team.

The last foreign coach I had was Jon Emmett, and this was the longest foreign coaching partnership that I had the privilege of learning from.

After reading his book *Be Your Own Sailing Coach* I approached him on Facebook. I asked him lots of questions regarding Laser Radial sailing because there was no coach in China who had sailed this class. I talk elsewhere in this book in more detail about Jon, together with the London Olympic Games.

In summary, all the foreign coaches had a positive role and

brought fresh blood into Chinese sailing as a whole. But they all suffered, more or less, from some unpleasant experiences while coaching the Chinese teams, particularly caused by the different habits, values and beliefs between the east and the west.

Interlude 3: Relationship with Coaches

Communication is the key!

As a Chinese I used to listen, obey and do everything that I heard, was instructed or taught. All Chinese are trained so well in the education system not to raise their voices, not to object, not to doubt, not to ask. I had to do all of these things even if I was unwilling or hated doing them.

However I am not the kind of girl who lets others control my life easily. I felt I must do something different to change my destiny. Gradually I was no longer seen as a 'good girl' in the team or even at home. I tried to do different things which I thought were better.

Some in China saw me as an alien who behaved in what they thought was a strange or even crazy way. I set effective training sessions myself; I ate food that provided more energy and nutrition; I did regeneration (active recovery from exercise) to help me recover quicker, and so on. In summary, I used all the knowledge that I had learnt from books, I asked experts and talked to specialists. I tried new things and was not afraid that some things might not work. That's how I grew up and progressed on an endless journey of self-discovery and self-improvement.

All of a sudden my life and career lit up when an Englishman called Jon Emmett started to coach me. He listened to me, talked with me, tried to understand me. He helped me minimise injuries and trained me to become an elite sailor. In the end, as you all know, he pushed me all the way to claim the Olympic gold medal in London in 2012.

He is one of the best Laser Radial sailing coaches in the world. His personality and style of coaching are near perfect. I am sure that anyone who has worked with him would share this view, and I am also pretty certain that he can really help sailors to maximise their potential and perform their best in the boat.

As athletes, I believe we should initiate communication with our coaches and leaders: letting them know about our feelings and worries, giving feedback and asking questions. We should discuss with them how to develop the best plan or solution.

Chapter 9

Getting to Grips with the Laser Radial

Less than eight months after first sailing the Laser Radial, I arrived in Los Angeles two weeks before the World Championship in July 2006. We planned to do some pre-event training in order to familiarise ourselves with a venue we had never been to before.

We went to the Laser equipment tent to collect our charter boats, but found we were not allowed to use the boats for training. We had not ticked the 'charter extension' option on the Laser website. We hadn't known about this and we had no idea what to do next. What was the use coming to a major regatta two weeks early with no boats to sail?

Luckily Ryan Eric Minth, who was our foreign coach at that time, managed to borrow five old boats from several local sailing clubs and so the six of us girls could sail in rotation each day. Ryan came just in time to teach us some basic skills in a Laser so that our speed could match the top of the fleet. Even so, I was still struggling with heavy wind steering and hiking.

Fortunately the whole event turned out to be a light and medium wind regatta, with only one strong wind race. Yet I can remember clearly (almost ten years later!) when the top-seeded local sailor, Paige Railey, rolled over me upwind in that race. I was totally astonished by her frequent adjustment of the mainsheet, sheeting in and out, whereas I was still holding the mainsheet in the clam cleat, as I used to in the Europe.

I was not upset by her overtaking me at all. I was delighted: I was close enough to observe her technique and felt as if I had won the lottery by having this unexpected discovery. The main cause of my disappointing speed in heavy wind finally came to light: I needed to play the mainsheet actively with the waves or chop in order to keep the boat flatter rather than tightening the sheet and sailing with the boat heavily heeled.

I sailed consistently throughout the regatta. Even though I did not win a single race, I was consistently in the top ten. To everyone's surprise, I won the whole event with a race to spare.

To be honest, I didn't feel that I deserved being crowned the Laser Radial World Champion that year. I knew that my level then was just around top ten and nowhere near top 3. It was because all the other top sailors had some bad races which put them out of contention. I felt I was just lucky. But I was very happy about the things that I had learnt through that event and the fact that winning this title meant that the leaders allowed me to do more international regattas.

Jon was leading the Men's World Championship in the first half of the regatta and we spoke briefly. At that time my English name was Lucy – chosen by my English teacher at primary school. I didn't like it much and so later changed it to Lily as this refers to the middle character of my Chinese name, and I really like the flower as well.

In terms of results I had a brilliant year in 2006. Within ten months of starting to sail the Laser Radial I had won the National Championship, Asian Games and World Championship. At the same time, however, the physically demanding boat challenged my body to such an extent that I had a series of injuries, one after another.

I was in continuous pain, day in and day out, from my leg which had been operated on. This left me unable to focus while training and I suffered insomnia. Many times it was so painful in the middle of the night that I got up and went outside so that I did not wake up my teammates. While wandering around outside, I would kick the wall hard to numb myself so that I wouldn't feel the pain temporarily. This was just a short and irrational solution to free myself from pain and suffering for a while.

Apart from this, both my knees felt like they had needles pinching inside them when I was hiking. The strange diagnosis was that this was simply because I have a naturally cold body with poor blood circulation towards my arms and legs. Once I get cold and wet on the water, my heart is not powerful enough to send blood all over my body. I often sail with numb hands and feet because I am cold, however much I wear. No wonder I always tend to be more sensitive to temperature than other people, and many of my friends describe me as a corpse when they touch my hands, knees or feet because they cannot believe how cold my extremities are. I still have not found a way of preventing or curing this.

I also hurt my lower back due to weak core muscle support and incorrect posture when hiking. After an MRT examination I was diagnosed with lumbar disc herniation. Instead of an operation, the doctor suggested a conservative therapy using a traditional Chinese treatment. Sixty silver needles, roughly ten times the size of acupuncture needles, were squeezed into my back, and then the therapist lit a fire to warm the needles, transferring heat into the deep tissues. This was by far the most frightening therapy I had ever experienced. The sharp pain made me cry for hours, and I tore the bed sheet when the doctor inserted those needles. I couldn't help shouting from the pain, losing my voice when I was pushed out of the treatment room on the trolley.

It was such a horrible experience but, after three days lying in bed, I did feel some recovery in my lower back. But it was a short term cure and I soon started to suffer from lower back pain again every day after sailing. I realised that I had better find a way to prevent the symptoms rather than having treatment after the pain occurred. However, none of the doctors or therapists in China were able to offer me sport-specific remedies, because they only deal with ordinary people, not sailors. At this stage I was not as lucky as westerners who have specialist sports therapists and fitness trainers guiding you in how to deal with such issues in a scientific way.

Sometimes I did complain that I was like a disabled woman: painful knees, sore left leg bone, lower back pain, loss of hearing, blurred left eye sight, vulnerable to cold, and so on. However, it was the news on the International Sailing Federation (ISAF) website about Paige Railey winning the Rolex World Sailor of the Year in 2006 that cheered me up and made me more determined. In her interview she said: "I compete in sailing because it's what I love to do. I believe it is a gift I have been granted, and I feel it is my obligation to take my gift to as high a level as I can. Sometimes, when my body is hurting after sailing, I ask myself if it is all worth it. It is on nights like tonight that I realise that it is all worth it."

Obviously it is not just me: most professional athletes unintentionally injure themselves from time to time. It is just an issue of how you deal with it. I have exactly the same emotion as Paige: sailing is something I want to do for my whole life, no matter what kind of difficulties I might encounter. I would never give up! So it's no use complaining about the injury, but face it boldly, deal with it effectively and then let it go positively.

Positive Affirmation 4: Super Health

I am a supremely healthy girl who treats herself with love and respect. I praise and bless every square inch of my body. I concentrate on the good things about me. I take time off for myself, fill myself up, and attend to my joy first, until I become a magnet of the universe.

I can get through injury easily, include laughter as part of my healing, watch funny movies and listen to nice music. Nothing is incurable but, if there is, it simply requires curing from within. I can change my life and I can cure myself. I was already healed and grateful for my healing. I see myself living in a perfectly healthy world, and let the doctor look after the wounds.

I can eat whatever I want and I am always the perfect weight. I reduce the amount I eat on rest days to give my stomach a rest.

I read and repeat this affirmation whenever and wherever I can.

Chapter 10

My First Olympics & the Build Up

The ISAF World Championship is held once every four years, with all ten Olympic classes racing at the same venue at the same time. This was held in Cascais, Portugal, in 2007 with the slogan "The Wind is Calling" – referring to the strong winds in that venue.

I improved my upwind speed throughout the year and was now able to match all the other top sailors in heavy conditions. I am also particularly good at sailing in big waves. These both contributed to my perfect start at this event with three firsts and a third. I was leading all the way until the final day before the Medal Race when a nightmare happened.

The conditions for the two races of that day were extremely tricky. There was an offshore wind, varying from 2 to 30 knots, with 60 to 90 degree wind shifts happening every two minutes! I had never sailed in such changeable conditions and completely lost myself, tacking with the frequent shifts. I sailed in a mess and had two results in the twenties. This dragged me from the top to tenth overall, but at least I could compete in the Medal Race (for the top ten), which was the only relief.

Despite this, I was genuinely pleased with my improvements in both upwind speed and downwind surfing, giving me confidence for the future challenge. I firmly believe that winning is about working harder, going longer and giving more than anyone else.

By 2008, two years after starting to sail the Laser Radial, my performance was becoming more and more consistent. I was regularly in the top three: winning Sail Melbourne, the New Zealand Nationals, Sail Auckland and Kiel Week; second in the World Championship; third in Lake Garda Olympic Week. My world ranking also rose to number two, with Anna Tunnicliffe from USA as number one.

However, the 2008 Olympic sailing venue, in Qingdao, is not one where I perform well. It has a renowned reputation of light wind, strong current and big waves. I love light conditions and am excellent in catching oscillating wind shifts, but in Qingdao it is mostly about sailing in the fast current. My weakest area was in downwind when the tide was going against the wind direction.

Sometimes the current was so strong that the whole fleet sailed parallel to each other, making the downwind leg look like a starting line. The last boat round the windward mark could overtake thirty boats and become the first one at the leeward mark. This is a unique feature of the sailing water in Qingdao, and quite often I failed to deal with it well. In the two Olympic Test Events, I only finished ninth and eleventh; not even among the top three hopefuls.

This was the situation before my home Olympic Games and I had no confidence about it at all. Nevertheless, I ignored this and did my best to prepare well. After so many years of training up to this point, I felt I should at least give my best performance, make the most of the situation and enjoy it!

I started the Olympics with a twenty-fourth in the first race and my coach was furious. I hate it whenever people shout at me.

Why couldn't we talk calmly and analyse the problem so that I could avoid making the same mistakes? Yelling or anger doesn't solve anything. However, I didn't let this negative behaviour ruin my preparation for the next race. Instead I returned to focus on my own sailing and the race.

Most of the races were in light winds apart from one strong and one medium wind race. I didn't even aim for the top three as I was completely honest with myself about the difficulties I had in this particular venue. All I did was concentrate on the things I had control over, and gave my all, without any regret.

Unexpectedly, I outperformed, grabbing some golden opportunities to catch up, and my overall standing gradually improved each day. Meanwhile, some Qingdao-specialist sailors were probably affected by 'Olympic pressure' and failed to perform as expected. So it was actually my rivals who 'awarded' me the Olympic bronze medal, while I miraculously survived the 'poisonous' pressure from the huge expectations of coaches, teams, family and friends, especially at a home Olympics.

The Olympic Games are something really special and different from all other competitions. You have got to prepare mentally as well as physically and in sailing techniques. Psychology plays an enormous role when you are under pressure and this is neglected by many athletes.

We all trained so hard, but some ended up failing to peak at the right time and, all of a sudden, those efforts were in vain. Don't wait 'til the crucial moment before realising the importance of mental control and start investing some time now into psychological drills and practice. This was the biggest lesson I learnt from my first Olympic Games.

Interlude 4: Mental Attitude

The sharpest edge is psychology and sailing is at least 80% mental. Try to have the same discipline in your mental practice as you have in your physical practice. By using mental training strategies, we can gain more control over what happens during important competitions by being completely prepared in mind, body, and spirit. The pictures in the mind determine the atmosphere of a person's world. So first of all, learn to see yourself as a winner and a competent athlete. The true joy comes from being fully present in each and every moment so focus your full attention on what's happening right at this moment! Think with your heart and recondition it into a positive and learning mode.

Our life is spent thinking. What we focus on and work on, we can create. The judgement begins within us, so why not let positive thinking be your guide? Only we have control over our own behaviour and the only behaviour that we can change is our own. Take control of your own life and don't rely on others to save you or to make things happen for you. Be an initiator, be proactive rather than reactive. That is to say, to initiate a play or move instead of waiting to respond. Take your time to enjoy, to learn, to experience each movement and moment. Have fun and enjoy your life. You can have fun but still be serious.

For the mental training to work best, we must practise it often. Be willing to take risks, to reach, and to move beyond old beliefs and fears that surround you. Do something new and let go of the worries about looking or feeling stupid. Be in the present moment and let go of the past, breathe in when you are tense or scared, have fun and enjoy, participate 100 percent without fear of failure.

Risk is the ability to take chances. Be willing to risk failure or lose face in order to surpass a record that stood for decades. Confront the fear instead of avoiding it. By letting ourselves be seen, by letting ourselves do something different, we grow. Sometimes the process of taking risks is as important as the outcome. By feeling calm and confident, we create a positive atmosphere. Be patient with yourself and trust the whole process: our team has helped us and our family or friends have supported us.

Whenever something goes wrong, accept it, let it go, and return your internal focus to the event. Use your performance as a learning experience. Remember to breathe slowly and deeply. Feel yourself being totally relaxed, confident and in complete control of both body and mind. Make an effort to breathe deeply and to create a more relaxed state of mind. Receive acknowledgement from others, be the master of your emotions, acknowledge the feelings and then drop them, refocus on the task in hand and stay in the present moment.

My views on this subject were influenced by *The Mental Athlete* by K Porter and *With Winning in Mind* by L R Bassham, which I highly recommend.

Chapter 11

A Slow Recovery

After the Beijing Olympics I stopped sailing and intensive training due to having too many injuries (although I did go to the World Championship every year either to see any developments or to race to retain some feeling of the boat, even though I was very unfit and rusty). While receiving treatment to help my body recover, I went to study at Shanghai Jiaotong University.

Meanwhile the desire to win an Olympic gold medal never stopped. There is a very limited amount of knowledge or information about sailing in China, so I searched for many English books on Amazon and the US Sailing and RYA (Royal Yachting Association, the UK sailing governing body) websites that are related to dinghy sailing or racing. The amount I spent on those books was equivalent to the annual salary for an ordinary Chinese person, as they are much more expensive due to international postage fees and the huge differences in living costs.

I remember how angry my parents were with me for spending so much money on books and they kept telling me: "the more you read, the more stupid you become". This was one of the famous mottos from our former Chairman Mao Ze Dong, and many of my parents' generation were big followers of him. (During the Cultural Revolution there were millions of books burned under Mao due to his fear of losing complete control over the population, and especially the threat from intellectuals.)

I couldn't help myself indulging in the richness of those books and the satisfaction of finding out something new and useful. Among all the English sailing books I read, *Be Your Own Sailing Coach* (the new edition is called *Coach Yourself to Win*) by Jon Emmett is the one that stood out the most. It combines both interesting diagrams and easy-to-understand demonstrations, and covers almost all the aspects dinghy sailors need to know to improve their competitiveness.

It not only helped me to understand more about sailing and theories in general, but also boosted my confidence and determination to train more scientifically, systematically and effectively in preparation for future competitions and campaigns.

By early 2010 I had decided to restart sailing, even though I wasn't fully recovered from the many annoying injuries. I planned to do the World Championship in Largs, Scotland that year, together with the Sail for Gold Regatta in Weymouth, England.

In order to find an excellent coach to help me campaign for London 2012, I searched for Jon Emmett on Facebook and got in contact with him. Even though I had never met or talked to him before, I was totally engaged and convinced by his book. In addition, as he was British and lived (and sailed a lot) in Weymouth, it would be perfect to have him giving me local knowledge about the 2012 Olympic venue.

Ironically, Jon replied that he had congratulated me in Los Angeles when I had won the Laser Radial World Championship in 2006 and we had talked for a few minutes afterwards. Shame on Lily! (I have long been troubled by my poor short term memory. I always carry a small notebook with me to jot down things that come into my mind, otherwise I would have forgotten to do an awful lot of important things.)

Luckily enough, Jon said that he would be able to coach me at Sail for Gold in 2010, but not at the World Championship in Largs as he would be competing himself. So we both started to prepare for our initial collaboration to see how we got on before deciding whether to sign a long term contract working towards the London Olympic Games.

At the same time, Rick Pointon, the founder of the Beijing Sailing Centre, was also trying to help the Chinese Sailing Team to find a foreign coach. Rick had moved to Beijing from the UK in early 2007. He couldn't find anywhere to go sailing and was missing the sport. He investigated the possibility of setting up a sailing centre to serve the Chinese market, especially the area around Beijing. A mutual friend had put us in contact and we arranged to have dinner at the Shangri-La Hotel in Qingdao in the summer of 2007 when he was attending a boat show. By the end of dinner, I felt we were firm friends and Rick said that he was fully prepared to do anything in his power to help me.

We remained in touch, mostly by e-mail. In February 2010 I mentioned that I was having difficulty finding a foreign coach for London 2012. Rick took this as a request for assistance and immediately set about talking to his UK contacts to see who might be appropriate. His Chief Instructor, Alfie Rowson, who had raced Lasers in the UK at a National level, suggested a few names, and also received input from Ian Walker. Ian is a double Olympic silver medallist, who also coached Shirley Robertson to an Olympic gold medal, and was, at the time, running a joint Irish-Chinese entry into the Volvo Ocean Race named Green Dragon.

The shortlist of potential coaches consisted of Mark Littlejohn, Hugh Styles, Jon Emmett, Steve Cockerill, Dave Cockerill and Mark Rushall. Rick and Alfie approached each of the candidates to determine their interest in the role, their availability and costs.

Rick subsequently emailed Yankee with the following:

- Mark Littlejohn: Still trying to get hold of him to see if he is available, but we think he is contracted to another squad already.
- Hugh Styles: Is interested and will forward his proposal.
- Jon Emmett: Is interested and available to coach your squad directly.
- Steve Cockerill: Just making initial contact.
- Dave Cockerill: Just making initial contact.

Hugh Styles provided a detailed proposal, but, in the end, it came to nothing and Jon Emmett was taken on, but not yet.

In July 2010 I went to the Laser Radial Worlds in Largs, underprepared as I was still struggling to train properly. Because of my severe lower back pain and knee issues, the doctor only allowed me to do physical training for half an hour a day. On the one hand, I was so eager to do more training and sailing in order to race well for these regattas, but on the other hand I was suffering a lot of pain throughout my body.

Nevertheless, I decided to stick to the original plan and race as much as I could while in the UK. Later it turned out to be a nightmare as I only managed to sail one race each day for the qualifying series in Largs. Although I failed to finish the regatta, it was still worth the effort to make the trip which gave me the chance to see the situation with the other international sailors –

how they'd sailed recently, how much they'd improved, any new faces and techniques coming up, and so on.

However this was far from an ideal way to recover from my injuries and it seemed better to continue my treatment, rather than risk things getting worse under the demanding fitness requirements of sailing a Laser. The team decided to send me back to China as soon as possible. Because of this I had to cancel Jon coaching me at Sail for Gold the following month.

We greeted each other in the café of Largs Sailing Club, while waiting ashore for a postponement. Obviously he was very disappointed about the sudden change of plan which also put him in an embarrassing position. He went to great lengths to demonstrate that he could help me solve my back problem, as well as other injuries, through Pilates exercise and physiotherapy. But unfortunately I had no choice but to fly home to see my doctor in Shanghai. Because of this, Jon didn't get his pay and lost one month's work which very nearly stopped him ever wanting to work with the Chinese again.

By then, all sorts of challenges lay ahead of me. When would I recover and be able to train competitively again? Would I have to face retirement after a long period of medical treatment? If I got back to sailing, would I ever have the chance to work with Jon, after the cancellation at short notice, which clearly damaged the credibility of the Chinese? Everything was uncertain at that stage.

2011 arrived quietly as I continued my treatment and studied at the University. My health seemed to get better when living as an ordinary person, and not as a professional athlete. My doctor suggested to me that, if I wanted to have good health for the rest of my life, I should retire and avoid the chronic symptoms which would seriously affect the rest of my life.

Even though I had got rid of the severe and intermittent pain after two years' treatment, it was not guaranteed that I could sustain the arduous training. Again I was left with two options which led in completely opposite directions: either study, then find a job and live healthily, with regret; or campaign for the London Olympic Games, which I might have to stop half way due to recurring injuries from intensive training, but at least without regret. I chose the second without hesitation. I knew that the price might well be high, and I certainly didn't want to suffer painful illnesses. But the fire inside my heart was so strong that I couldn't accept giving up without a final attempt. Even if there was only 1% of hope, I was prepared to face any outcome or consequence.

I returned to the National Sailing Team in February 2011, planning to do my first international regatta in Hyeres, France, in April, followed by a programme of training and racing around Europe. Meanwhile I contacted Jon Emmett again, hoping that he would give me a second chance of working together. Much to my delight, he generously accepted my invitation, but he already had a programme of work lined up. The first possible time slot in his schedule would be on 15th June, after the Sail for Gold regatta that year. We agreed to start in Weymouth and the first coaching period would be two months – all the way up to the Olympic Test Event.

I gradually increased my training load in February and March, while in China, and was ultra-cautious not to aggravate my body with the physical challenge. Even then things didn't seem any brighter as too often I needed three days' rest and therapy to recover from one heavy training session which triggered muscle spasm in my lower back. This made my return-to-sailing journey extremely difficult as it was almost impossible to make any progress under that training regime.

I was too unfit and vulnerable to injury to do a proper regatta after arriving in Hyeres that spring, so I decided to observe the racing, instead of sailing myself. I remember that I only managed to go on the water to watch the racing twice because even a few hours in a RIB aggravated my lower back problem, and I had to do numerous therapies to recover from it. The treatment was not pleasant or calm. Some days I couldn't help shouting and crying due to the painful needles of traditional Chinese medicine, other times I even tore the sheet and bit the pillow. Swallowing my tears, I looked at the sky and said in my mind: "Come on god, I will conquer every ordeal you throw at me, you'll see!"

After the Hyeres World Cup event I followed the team transferring to Lake Garda in Italy for the next training camp before the Olympic Week regatta. All of the team staff took great care of me and I started to test sail the Laser for half an hour a day, then forty-five minutes and gradually up to an hour. With careful evaluation from the doctor, and a flexible training plan designed for my body on a day-to-day basis, my back and knees gradually got stronger and tougher, and I could sustain heavy training for longer periods before pain and spasm reappeared. With all the assistance and support, I managed to do one race a day throughout a week's competition.

Next came the Medemblik World Cup in Holland and then Sail for Gold in the UK immediately afterwards. I finished all races with great effort. Despite the fact that I wasn't at all competitive, due to lack of fitness for the Radial class, I was very pleased to be back in the boat again. I felt sure that, as long as I could continue the progressive training and sailing, I would have the ability and skill to beat all my rivals. Those obstacles only served to motivate me even more and cherish every precious second with my dear sailboat.

Interlude 5: Dealing with Injury

Acknowledge the injury and have a conversation with the injured body part – ask the injury what it wants from you, and make a commitment to give it what it wants; ask it what it wants to tell you: to rest, to be mothered, to be iced, to get a massage, to relax, not to stretch it too hard, etc. Reply to it that it has been heard; get a massage and be gentler, slow down and release the stress in your life.

Open your heart to the pain, to injured feelings, to thoughts, and to dreams. Open up to the pain instead of resisting it. Concentrate and focus on your body as a whole, not on the specific area that feels tired or painful. See it as an opportunity to display courage and welcome it as a relief from the strenuous training, the drudgery of practice, and embarrassment and frustration of poor performance.

Forgive the injured part and the body as a whole. Stop worrying, instead imagine the injury getting better. Learn to take time for yourself and let go of the guilty feeling for taking that time. When we use our imagination, mental pictures and suggestion, we can make our body respond. Regard it as a friend to be helped and healed rather than an enemy to be resented or feared. We have nothing to lose and much to gain by joining in this experiment of self-healing.

My views on this subject were influenced by *The Mental Athlete* by K Porter and *With Winning in Mind* by L R Bassham, which I highly recommend.

Chapter 12

Finally Teaming Up with Jon Emmett

After Sail for Gold in 2011, Jon Emmett joined the Chinese Sailing Team, coaching the Laser Radial squad. At that time we had five top girls from different provinces in China training together. Since the rest of the sailors and coaches in the National Team barely spoke any English, I took the role of being a translator for Jon, to communicate with all the other Chinese.

Jon introduced us Radial girls to many new, interesting and effective types of training. We never thought, or had experienced, that training can also be fun and enjoyable. Most of the time when we trained with Chinese coaches the atmosphere was stale and repetitive, feeling like prisoners being forced to do something reluctantly. The coaches always wore a straight face and shouted or criticised us for not doing this or that. With Jon it was completely the opposite: we had laughs and received cheerful remarks in every training session. I remember some of the things my teammates said to me: "I've started to enjoy sailing now, I wish I could have met Jon earlier"; "He really listens to sailors and takes our feeling and feedback into consideration"; "Instead of telling us what to do, Jon explains to us why and helps us to understand and think for ourselves"; "He knows exactly what we sailors need and want the most, because he still sails and races competitively himself'".

*

I guess by now you will have some idea how boring we Chinese athletes are: we have to train in the team all year round and have only one holiday a year, for a period of one or two weeks, back home with our families. We have no freedom to choose what we would like to do, but have to follow and obey what is set out by our coaches or leaders. We are afraid to voice our opinions as such behaviour is likely to be criticised or punished. We have no opportunities to socialise as we are not allowed to see our family and friends while in the team. Even the time using computers and the internet is limited and we have to comply with many of the team rules such as: roll call in the evening; handing over computers and cutting off the internet before bed; lights off at 10pm (9pm when I was sailing an Optimist); no boyfriends or girlfriends before the age of 25; asking for permission to leave the team building (if you want to go to the town, for instance); to name a few. Does this sound to you like we are in a well-ordered and controlled military life? Or even worse than soldiers in other countries?

*

Well, let's get back to Jon's coaching, apart from all those exciting training experiences he brought to us, he also introduced me to Pilates in order to solve my lower back problem. At first I could hardly believe that those weird breathing methods and small muscle group exercises could have the effect of curing my spine

"I was born in 1987 in Shanghai, the largest city in China. Five of us shared a two bedroom flat... My grandparents lived in one room, while I shared the other room with my parents."

1988 *My grandparents doted on me when I was a baby. I wish that they could have seen me achieve all that I have done today*

2005 *The roles began to reverse as I grew up. Here I am with my grandparents, aged 18*

1989 *Here I am one year and ten months old. Maybe covering my ears was my way of communicating my hearing difficulties...*

1990 *Three years old. Standing tall and proud in my very first dress!*

"My mother cried for several nights on end as she couldn't accept that I would be leaving home for a long time. I had been her life from when she was pregnant, through giving birth to me and over the ten years she brought me up, and all of a sudden she could no longer be with me."

1997 *With my mother at the Shanghai Water Sports Centre at the start of my sailing career*

2001 *A few years later... here I am aged fourteen*

"My father said, "Lily, this is the road you chose yourself. So whenever or whatever hardship confronts you, you must keep marching bravely ahead and never give up!"

2005 *A very proud father, posing in front of some of my medals and certificates*

2007 *Aged 20, the precious once-a-year holiday after the Olympic test event in Qingdao*

"On seeing a poster for a district swimming team outside my pre-school front gate, [my parents] sent me to see a swimming coach, which was followed by some test exercises. Luckily I was accepted by the Changning District Swimming team of Shanghai. So my sports career started at the age of 5."

1993 *Aged 6, after my first swimming competition*

"What is sailing?" I asked.
"It's steering a boat on the water. Why not give it a try: you may well love it and not want to get off the boat afterwards."

1997 *My first year in an Optimist. I became a full-time sailor not long after my 10th birthday*

1998 *Winning the Optimist National Championship in Hong Kong. It was here that I was awarded my very first medal in sailing*

2000 *"I gave all I had and shared everything with Echo." From 'master' and 'apprentice' blossomed a lasting friendship; Echo and I maintain a good relationship to this day*

2002 *I concluded my Optimist career aged 15 by winning the Asian Games in Busan, Korea*

"Only two weeks after I competed in my last Optimist event at the Asian Games, I went to Hainan for the National Championship of the Europe class, which was then the Olympic single-handed dinghy for women."

2005 *With my foreign coach from France at the Europe National Championship (I'm top right)*

2005 *Winning the Europe National Championship*

"Once you are in the army training, you must comply with every instruction and have no right to say a single 'no'."

2005 *Before commencing training in the Laser Radial class, I was required to attend a two-week army training camp*

2005 *ISAF Youth World Championship. My first touch of a Laser Radial*

2006 Asian Games Laser Radial
open class. I was crowned
champion, with all other
participants being male

2007 ISAF World Championship,
Cascais, Portugal. I led all the
way until the final day before
the Medal Race, ending up
finishing the championship in
tenth place

"The Olympic Games are something really special and different from all other competitions."

2008 *My first Olympic Games, held in my home country. I competed in the women's Laser Radial class at the sailing venue in Qingdao, and was awarded the bronze medal*

2008 *Gintarė Volungevičiūtė-Scheidt from Lithuania (right) won silver, and Anna Tunnicliffe from the United States (centre) was awarded the gold medal*

"In order to find an excellent coach to help me campaign for London 2012, I searched for Jon Emmett... I was totally engaged and convinced by his book."

2012 *Jon and I teamed up for my Olympic campaign, and we remain great friends today*

2012 Olympic Games, London. "This race was going to be a fierce competition."

"I managed to protect my leading position all the way to the finish by combining tactics with playing the shifts."

"I kissed my boat and thanked her for her cooperation and company on this wonderful journey."

Celebrating with my fellow Olympic medallists: Marit Bouwmeester of Netherlands (left) won silver and Evi Van Acker of Belgium (right) took bronze

2012 *ISAF Rolex World Sailor of the Year Awards. I was honoured to be crowned Female Sailor of the Year, alongside Male Sailor of the Year, Sir Ben Ainslie*

Since becoming an Olympic gold medallist and Rolex World Sailor of the Year 2012, my life has certainly not slowed...

2013 *As BMW are one of my sponsors I was invited to the BMW Masters opening night in Shanghai, alongside Rory McIlroy and Peter Hanson*

2015 *Volvo Ocean Race. I was a Team SCA Ambassador and onboard guest, and was given the opportunity to jump off the boat at the start of Leg 4*

problems. But after some time, when I was able to undertake more and more intensive training without suffering any pain, I had no reason to doubt the function and usefulness of Pilates any more. I had never dreamt of sailing without annoying injuries – what a blessing!

Jon is also an expert in physical training and helped me improve my weakest areas in fitness. He not only coached and sailed with us, but also did gym work and cycling as a training partner. Thanks to his years of experience sailing in Weymouth, he imparted a great deal of valuable information about the Olympic venue. A solid fourth overall in the Test Event in August 2011 clearly showed how much I had progressed in the previous two months through training with Jon, especially considering that it was less than four months since I returned to sailing after two years away from proper training due to injuries.

This first collaboration with Jon proved to be a great success and this sent a positive message to my leaders that Jon would be the perfect coach to assist me in winning a gold medal at the London Games. So a long term contract was signed between the Chinese Sailing Team and Jon. But both Jon and I were completely unaware of how difficult and challenging the year ahead of us would be. The storm was yet to come...

*

Not long after the 2011 Olympic Test Event, Jon flew to China to start the long term contract with the Chinese Laser Radial Team. Unlike other Chinese sports teams, which are all based at the National Training Centre in the heart of the capital city, Beijing, the National Sailing Team usually set up training camps in different places in Southern China using the provincial team's base and facilities.

That year Jon joined us in Dongshan, a small town in Fujian province. It is so remote that you can barely find any big shops or entertainment, let alone cinemas or pubs. I do wonder what Jon's first impression was when he arrived in such a backward rural area after settling down in a dilapidated building. The way people dressed, ate and behaved must have been very strange to him. However, there were many other culture shocks that Jon would experience and lessons he would learn during his stay in China.

First there was the notorious Chinese drinking tradition. It is quite a common routine for most Chinese leaders and coaches to drink every evening, whether it be a formal dinner or a late night get-together. It wouldn't be such a bad thing for those who enjoy drinking, but the need to do 'bottoms-up' (drain your glass) to show your sincerity towards another person must have trapped a great number of people.

And so it was for Jon: he unavoidably got drawn into every day's drinking game with other members of the Chinese team staff including leaders, coaches, doctors, chefs and so on. They enjoyed persuading Jon to drink different types of strong Chinese alcohol. As Jon put it, those Chinese drinking adults are more or less like British teenagers or university students who indulge themselves in pubs and parties and have almost no self-control or discipline to avoid getting drunk.

But in China, if you want to remain in a good social or working relationship with others, especially the leaders, you have to prove your genuine respect by lots of one-on-one 'Gan Bei's (bottoms-up) and toasts. If you only drink casually, in the volume you want, then you would not only lose your 'business' but also have no chance of getting a 'yes' from the leaders when you want them to approve you doing something.

It may seem ridiculous, but Jon had to accompany them drinking almost every night to keep all the Chinese happy, so that he got the best possible training programme, facilities and equipment for us sailors. Otherwise the leaders would have denied everything Jon asked for and even started to distrust him. So, when Jon joined the Chinese Sailing Team, he had to train and coach the sailors during the day and then drink with the leaders in the evening.

Now you can imagine how demanding it is for a foreigner to coach the Chinese team. Jon had to deal with insufficient sleep as well as improper recovery from intensive training and the demanding coaching role. All he wanted was to do a good job for the sailors and provide us with the best opportunity to improve our sailing. I clearly remember in some early morning training sessions, I could smell the strong alcohol coming from Jon. He would have had only a few hours' sleep, but still he insisted on running and cycling with all the sailors for two hours or so. On other days, during sailing sessions, he accidentally capsized or hit himself with the boom while on the water. He was indeed trying extremely hard to adapt himself to this alien eastern culture.

Another classic phenomenon about China that seemed unbelievable to Jon was the absolute hierarchical control. All the sailors have to listen unconditionally to their coaches; the coaches obey their leaders; and the leaders report to their superiors. What Jon found hard was how those leaders, who had never sailed, could say that they knew what was best for the sailors and arrange everything based on their knowledge of an unrelated realm. They were unwilling to listen to the sailors' opinions and it was a common practice to deny or disagree with what some-one in a lower position said or asked for. So however hard the sailors tried to make the most reasonable and sensible sugges-tions to their coaches and leaders, their effort was mostly in vain.

Keeping face is another speciality of China. One is justified telling lies in order to save face. People don't feel guilty about, or realise the seriousness of losing credibility from, dishonest state-ments and actions. In an effort to control those of a lower status, they would try to keep the sailors in the dark, not letting them know what was happening or going to happen. Those of a lower status are like frogs in a well: they have no idea of what it is like in the outside world and accept, or even believe, that the sky is just the size they can see from the well.

In China, sailors have no rights to set their own training pro-grams and racing plans, nor are they allowed to choose what they really want; they have to listen, obey, follow and copy. No socialising with friends, no time with families, no studies to con-tinue to educate themselves and no basic human rights such as equality, democracy or freedom. What matters most to the leaders is just how many hours we train a week, a month, a sea-son, and what results we can get from competitions. The leaders firmly believe that accumulated long hours of training are the most crucial – and the only necessity – for success, with racing being a very distant second.

But sailing involves fleet control and boat-on-boat tactics. It is not the same as rowing or swimming, where it is solely about technique and speed. Those leaders who deny the importance and usefulness of regattas know little about sailing, but regard themselves as experts in all sports. In their minds practice regattas are unnecessary and the only thing that makes any difference is lots of hard training. In the early years, I only got the chance to do two or three events per year. That's close to what British sailors would compete in every month! Rather, Chinese sailors had to train every season, for more than 300 days a year, with no holidays, no family time and no study: just like birds in a cage, or slaves in a prison – machines doing the same job every single day.

Another fact that both Jon and I found difficult was the Chinese habit of changing things and not thinking or planning ahead. For instance, before Jon came to Dongshan, he was told to fly to Shanghai and then transfer to Xiamen. So he bought a non-refundable ticket to save money. Later the team changed their mind and asked him to buy an entirely new ticket, and they never reimbursed him for the previous one.

All too often the sailors don't know what the next plan is in terms of training or trips and end up just playing games, surfing the internet or watching television to kill time waiting for the next instruction to come through. This is a deeply rooted approach to deliver a simple, stable and easy life instead of a challenging, but more meaningful, one.

For me, all of this is just part of my nation's culture; a result of the long, rich Chinese history, complicated by political factors. The atmosphere and environment where I grew up cultivates the accepting and following nature of the majority of Chinese people, as well as their overly-respectful attitude towards the power of leaders, love of important sounding titles and only doing things in their own interest. The pursuit of superficial things leads many Chinese away from the true values of life.

However, in spite of all these things, there are still many positive things about China: if there is something the Chinese want to achieve, nothing can block this mighty nation. Economically it already leads the world, but the quality of life and the average living standard is yet to improve.

Positive Affirmation 5: Olympic Champion

I am the 2012 World Sailing Championship Laser Radial Class Gold Medallist, the best female athlete of Chinese sports and World Sailor of the Year. Sailing under the union flag, receiving a gold medal and hearing the national anthem being proudly played is the best and most exhilarating experience in my career. I have taken my next step toward the accomplishment of my lifelong goal – becoming an Olympic champion.

I enjoy the recognition I get as one of the best sailors in the world. I love being on the water in all conditions and am keen to perform the best I can in my sport. When I am racing, I commit my all, body and soul, and nothing else matters. I control every element I am able to and have zero tolerance of anything else. I get my own preparation right, leave nothing to chance and take nothing for granted. I am ultra-cautious about the rules and play it safe all the time. I keep my composure, stay quietly confident and think radically at crucial junctures. I am good at dealing with all kinds of problems and not letting them affect my performance in any way.

I am very physical and ultra-aggressive once I hit the water, but a really nice girl and revert to my normal self and daily routines when on land. I train hard in the gym and sail smart on the water. Now I am incredibly fit, highly motivated and extremely well prepared – I know clearly I am here to win. I am at my peak and my body can withstand the rigour that is to come.

All my preparation has been designed to convince my opponents that they are fighting for Silver. I always run a mental programme before each racing day and reinforce each successful leg by saying: "THAT'S LIKE ME!" I record my performance analysis, and read and visualise my positive affirmation daily.

I am the National Games, World Championship, and World Cup Champion of the women's Laser Radial class sailing. Go on Lily, go for it. I know I have the edge.

Chapter 13

The Cracks Begin to Show

After the first training camp with Jon for two months, we headed to Melbourne, Australia, for the Sail Melbourne World Cup as a warm up event prior to the ISAF World Championship in Perth, Australia, in December 2011. Sail Melbourne was the first regatta I had won since teaming up with Jon and we both started to gain more confidence and our working together was becoming more interdependent and harmonious.

In theory, all the members of the Chinese Team should have been pleased by my massive progress with Jon's help. However, this was not the case for Lima. He was coaching the Laser boys in Melbourne and decried my result by remarking that the gold was won by my opponents' not taking it seriously, rather than by my good performance. I cannot remember everything and exactly when or why Lima started to turn against Jon, but he disagreed with almost everything related to this foreign coach and denied Jon's contribution to my performance. My best guess is that the tension may have resulted from jealousy and feeling threatened by somebody else.

Firstly, Jon's daily wage was similar to an average Chinese monthly salary. Some may have been envious of how much he earned compared to them. Most of the Chinese coaches and leaders undoubtedly felt overshadowed by Jon's coaching skills, covering a wide range of areas such as physical training, meteorology, psychology, logistics and sailing itself. They could not explain the reasons behind a certain theory or fact and would never discuss it with the sailors.

Secondly, as a British person, Jon is very honest and earnest with everything he says or does, and he would challenge lies or incorrect statements made by the coaches or leaders to their faces. Jon would object to things that they got wrong, reasoning with them with strong evidence. This severely damaged their 'face', which Chinese people care about so much. Someone who challenged and suggested something different was unlikely to be welcomed by the leaders or coaches. They enjoy the feeling of being above people and strictly controlling them to do as they said. That is why, as Chinese athletes, we are trained to keep silent and just accept and do things we are told to do, even if we are extremely unwilling.

Thirdly, I think that they felt uncomfortable seeing Jon and the sailors getting on particularly well, because he listens, discusses and is open and fair to all the sailors. We were dedicated and focussed while training, but could also laugh and joke like friends afterwards. This is not common between Chinese coaches and sailors, because they always have a serious and straight face in front of us, who are below them in status.

All of these things together, gradually, seemed to have built a dislike of Jon. As a result, the Chinese leaders were only going to make his job harder and tougher.

Morality, courtesy and fairness are all virtues I think China needs to improve upon when working internationally. To give you another example, originally we were planning to do the

Sydney International Regatta before the one in Melbourne. So Jon arranged all of the logistics for the trip: charter boats in excellent condition and accommodation right by the venue. All of a sudden, the team decided to cancel with no reason. They didn't care about the cost to others.

On another occasion, Lima was stopped by a policeman while driving on a motorway in Australia. He was fined for speeding and not wearing his seatbelt. The following day, on the way to the sailing club, we got pulled over again and Lima was nearly arrested, resulting in the sailors nearly missing the race. Most Chinese people are not in the habit of wearing a seatbelt, whether they are drivers or passengers. They don't take safety precautions seriously in many ways: coaches won't wear lifejackets, nor use kill cords (to stop the engine if they fall out); cyclists won't wear helmets or carry lights when it's dark. Comfort seems more important than safety and there is a reluctance to think of the bigger picture.

Another 'interesting' experience we had in Melbourne was on the rest day when we had decided to visit the famous Twelve Apostles (rock stacks that rise from the ocean on Victoria's coast). We got up early for the long drive and Lima drove to a petrol station to fill up, but he went to the petrol pump rather than the diesel one. Some of the sailors wondered why he chose petrol instead of diesel, but everyone was far too scared to tell him that he might be wrong. Jon told him, but was ignored and the van was wrongly filled up with petrol. This resulted in hours wasted in the petrol station to resolve the problem, while we walked home and waited. Fortunately the problem was solved by midday and we got to see the stunning Twelve Apostles, but only for a short time.

One day in Melbourne the Radial class was racing after the Lasers. Lima just followed the Chinese men back to the harbour and drove them to the hotel, leaving me, Jon and Echo to run back after finishing our race. This happened again in Perth when he didn't want to wait for me to get changed at the venue and so I ended up changing in a moving van since our rented house was nearly an hour away.

By the time we transferred from Melbourne to Perth, things got worse. My preparation before the most crucial event in 2011 (the World Championship) turned out to be a real mess and deeply upsetting.

We had a team meeting with all the team members regarding our pre-worlds training programme. Zulu and Lima simply refused the complete programme presented by Jon. They put forward excuses of a tight budget to not cover the gym fees and bike rentals, and would not agree with the daily schedule of sailing and fitness training.

For the first time in my life, I spoke up in front of all the team staff, saying that this sudden change was unreasonable before the biggest regatta of the year. Lima immediately dismissed me, saying how rude I was talking to them like that, and followed with a stream of criticism, blame and abuse. I felt so humiliated by Lima that I couldn't help bursting into tears:

"I am not a tourist here, just to have fun and waste time. I am here for the simple reason that I am giving 100% to campaign to be an Olympic Champion!"

"Shut up! Who the hell do you think you are talking to? From today onwards you are not allowed to train with the team anymore!"

Lima was indeed serious about what he said and, for almost

a month, he didn't say a word to me. I don't know how I got through that hard period. I could hardly believe that this terrible scenario had happened just before the World Championship. The obstacles were not from outside, but from within the team – what an absurdity!

I was cut off from everything related to training and Lima restricted me wherever he had control. The only good thing left for me was that I had Jon's support: "Don't worry Lily, we just do the best we can. Every cloud has a silver lining and we won't let this knock us down easily. Now it is the time for Jon and Lily to boldly march forward together!"

The following day Jon and I went to the bike shop, rented two road bikes, and paid the gym fees ourselves. We managed to do early fitness sessions the moment the gym opened in the morning, while the others were still sleeping. We took buses to the venue and used another teammate's boat to sail when the team had finished sailing.

This was the situation right before my big competition and the regatta wasn't any easier for me. Jon wasn't allowed to use another RIB which was in the container; he had to go on the water with Lima who drove the RIB as far away from me as possible.

Many times before the start I didn't have enough time to sail to them and drop my waterproof jacket off with them, so I just had to throw it to some other coaches in a hurry. Jon tried very hard to hire a RIB himself from local sailing clubs, but it was just impossible at such short notice with thousands of dinghies racing at the same time. Since Lima didn't let Jon talk to me on the water, the only time I could communicate with him was onshore, before and after racing.

However hard I tried to adjust my mood and face the adversities positively, my performance still suffered enormously. I found it extremely difficult to concentrate fully and struggled to get in the right mind-set for racing. All my effort went into trying to erase the terrible memory of the atmosphere in the team during that regatta. I wasn't surprised when I nearly failed to qualify for the Olympics, but I narrowly made the gold fleet in the final series. 'Messy' – the only word I can use to describe that regatta.

After the event Jon tried to console and cheer me up by saying: "Lily, what doesn't kill you makes you stronger. Let's face the challenge and fight for a bright future together, hand in hand."

Those simple words were encouraging and motivating. It was with Jon's assistance that I transformed myself from dependent to independent; but the best outcome was becoming interdependent. Armed with good communication and cooperation with Jon, together with the ultimate goal of the Olympics, I actually gained more confidence despite the setbacks I had experienced so far.

"I'm not going to give up. I will come back with a new, stronger, more determined Lily. Let's see!" I said to myself, deep inside my heart.

Would the situation get better? Only time would tell.

In Melbourne I had the first chance to race internationally with Jon as my coach. I wanted to do my best. In one of the races I came into the start on port, hit a starboard boat and just sailed on. Luckily there was a general recall otherwise I would probably have been protested. After the racing Jon quietly took me aside and talked to me about being consistent. He explained that I didn't need to win the start to win the race and I didn't need to win lots of races to win a championship. He also pointed out that I had knowingly and deliberately broken the rules. When I really thought about it I was so ashamed that I cried.

Previously I had had lots of OCS (on course side: i.e. over the line at the start) as a result of always trying to get the best start, rather than just a good one. Jon explained that consistency was the key. Possibly the fact that I was cut off from Jon in Perth resulted in two black flags (disqualified for being over the line at the start) and a disqualification as a result of a port-starboard incident. Old habits are hard to break, but we worked on this when we had a fresh start in the New Year.

While still in Australia, after the regatta in Perth, Jon tried his best to calm me. We did some touring and were able to talk freely, although the team tried to stop this by giving Jon jobs to do. One day we had booked a ferry to the island of Rottness where we did a gentle cycle and recovery and visited a light-house. In an attempt to stop this happening, Jon was asked to load the container, but he did the work very quickly and drove fast so that we just made the ferry in time. On another occasion we visited Freemantle prison and Jon found it somewhat ironic when he was asked to take a photo of me in that building. It was only when we were away from the team that I felt free and could relax and think clearly as we began to prepare for the difficult road ahead.

When we got back to China we worked very hard – even training on Christmas Day – just the two of us. The clock was ticking and we were determined to do our best.

Jon always tried to be gentle with me and took time to des-cribe the changes we were making and why. We had some quiet chats about changing the old Lily (bad habits) into a new Lily (transformed into good habits). The process was like a caterpillar gradually becoming a beautiful butterfly. Many people couldn't help noticing how much I changed working with Jon. After the Olympic Games he gave me a present of a framed real butterfly which I now hang on the wall and see every day.

Meanwhile Jon tried to seek help from Rick Pointon. In an email he wrote: "I do not think that I can continue with the job. The working conditions are completely impossible. Please let me know some of the top Chinese leaders' email addresses and I'll send them my report tomorrow. In the current system I simply cannot help Lily. I am blocked in everything I try to do, so it is pointless. I am deeply disappointed about this. The problem is the more time I spend with Lily one-to-one to help her, the more angry Lima gets and this really affects Lily. I am sure the results would have been different if I was allowed to do as planned. Anyway, I believe that by being here I actually make things worse for her. So if things do not change, it is best that I leave. I just want to do what is best for Lily. I can email her a physical training programme, what she needs to know about regattas. I have kept all this from her as she needs to be fully focussed on her campaign towards the Olympics."

Later Rick replied to Jon with some of the contacts he had at the Chinese Yachting Association. Jon wrote to every one of them in the hope of finding someone powerful enough to make a change to the current team situation.

After Perth, the team stopped paying Jon's salary regularly. At one point, the team owed him £26,000 and he could have easily refused to work any longer. Jon stayed because he really wanted to help me win an Olympic gold medal.

*

Early in August 2011 Rick was visiting friends in the UK and paid a visit to the Chinese Sailing Team's training camp at the Little Sea Caravan Park in Weymouth where we had the chance to catch up. It was great to see him again and we chatted away like long lost friends.

Recently Rick has provided his account of this time:

"2011 was a great year for the Beijing Sailing Centre, winning the China Cup and many other national events. But Jon was finding it hard living and working inside the Chinese State system. I did my best to support him and we became good friends. My experience of China is limited compared to Jon's, but we would spend late nights talking on the phone, meeting up and discussing ways to improve or address the training.

Jon is a very honourable man, with a very acutely defined set of morals. So when he felt the system was not right, or the training was not fully effect-ive, he just had to go on about it until he got some action. Sometimes I felt he needed a sounding board to vent some of his frustration at the variations from what he deemed to be the optimal training road.

In particular, he was sensitive as to how much he could burden Lily with these frustrations, so he seemed to welcome the opportunity to vent to me. I remember one night he was passing through Beijing and he stayed over at my house. We stayed up all night chatting about how it was like trying to train for a gold medal with one hand tied behind your back.

It was at this time that we devised the Lily Report as a method of sharing issues outside the team to the highest level. Each month Jon would prepare a report and send it out to the top people in the Chinese Yachting Association to say how training was going and what needed to be fixed. I'm sure it didn't win him any friends, but he did report positive action, such as the bikes in the squad gym being fixed.

Jon was as determined as Lily, and together I felt they made a very strong team. Not only was he extremely sensitive to using physical training to address imbalances within her core, but he seemed to give her the right confidence in sailing her own race. This was just an impression from afar, but I've no doubt that Jon was the wisest choice to coach Lily.

So that's the story as I recall it. One of the things that has always really impressed me about Lily is her humility. Even now that she is a Chinese sailing superstar, whenever we meet she always comes across as the girl next door and a good friend. I'm glad I was able to contribute in a small way towards her success, though all the hard work was hers alone."

Positive Affirmation 6: Core Performance

I use a Core Performance programme to meet my life's challenges. It consists of CORE MINDSET, NUTRITION, MOVEMENT and RECOVERY. I establish my core values, centred self and take a proactive approach with long term health as my first priority.

I eat six small to medium meals, every 2-3 hours, containing a combination of lean protein, healthy fats, and high-fibre organic carbohydrates – spread evenly across the day to regulate my blood sugar level which improves concentration and controls my appetite. I am accustomed to consuming smaller portions and listen to my stomach's response. I add a pre-workout starter or post-workout recovery mix to assist muscle repair. I avoid HFCS, saturated and trans fats, and remove the skin or fatty pieces from meat.

I have a strong, perfect posture throughout the day by pulling my shoulders back towards my back pockets, tummy in tight and fire my gluteus to initiate any movements. Every time I move, walk, or bend, I squeeze those hip muscles, my toes point straight ahead and my chest is over my knee. I build a straight line from ear to ankle. Feeling tall and stabilised through my pillar, I create a body that is resistant to injury, deterioration and excruciating back pain. I look for every opportunity to lengthen and strengthen my gluteus and use them constantly.

I cultivate a positive lifestyle based on core values, physical activity, and healthy eating that will fuel me toward success in every aspect of my life. I fully use what god and my parents gave me, to the best of my ability, through hard work, passion, honesty, and courage to lead the life that I've dreamed of – in a consistent pursuit of greatness. Live longer and better. The progress is unlimited.

I am irreplaceable! It's all about the power of my gluteus, how incredible it is! I look great, and more importantly, I feel great inside and out!

Chapter 14

Getting Better... Then Worse

In early 2012, for the first and only time, I did the Miami World Cup event in the United States. In order to get more freedom to coach me better, Jon managed to contact Quebec – the top leader in charge of Chinese sailing. Quebec showed his understanding of the situation we were in and guaranteed Jon the right to drive the RIB in Miami, as well as deciding the training plan for me only (not the other Radial girls). He didn't want to embarrass Lima's position as a head coach and so kept him in charge of the rest of the sailors.

So the moment we arrived in Miami, Jon and I went to find a gym nearby and rented road bikes ready for pre-regatta training. From hours of discussion we made out an ideal schedule which would maximise the quality of training, together with adequate recovery. The other sailors were free to choose whether to train with us, but they were not so keen on physical training, so we only sailed together on the water, leaving Jon and me to do our own fitness programme.

Everything was just so much better: quality training, proper preparation, effective communication and the satisfaction of improving a little bit every single day.

I am a big fan of racing, but not really that much of training. But during this period, for the first time ever, I found that training, both on the water and in the gym, could be fun. I felt so happy with everything. I strived to give 100% to train hard, to focus fully on the task at hand, in a peaceful state of mind, and enjoyed every second.

I recall that several foreign sailors came up to me and said that they had never seen me laugh or smile that much in the boat park before. Sport, for Chinese athletes, is nothing to do with fun, but rather a way to escape from boring school work or to earn money to support their poor families. I was one of the lucky ones who truly loved my sport, whereas the majority saw it as an obligation and wanted to retire as soon as possible. One of the sad things about former Chinese sailors was that, once they retired, they never wanted to touch a boat again as they had so many terrible memories and hated anything related to sailing.

Since China is such a controlled country, the moment you joined, or were selected, for a certain team, you were asked to sign a contract for four or eight years. You could be threatened that everything would be cut off if you retired, even at the end of the contract. You were told over and over again that, apart from sailing and training with the team, there is nothing else that you can do once you leave the team. So many, even though they wanted to leave the team, were 'forced' to continue 'servicing' the team until they were over 30 years old. Many female sailors have delayed having children simply to obey the team's command.

On the one hand you got paid a salary and all your expenses were covered, but on the other hand you were employed like a slave who had no freedom. The senior leaders did not realise that only happiness could make sailors want to stay longer and put more effort in.

After the training in Miami came the real contest. It was a relatively light wind regatta and I managed to win some match racing scenarios with Marit Bouwmeester from the Netherlands, who had just been crowned World Champion in Perth the previous month. Winning overall didn't give me that much delight because I know that I am a light wind specialist and my weakness was fitness which hindered my strong wind performance. Nevertheless, the top three sailors in Miami turned out to be exactly the same as at the Olympics: Lily, Marit and Evi.

The 2012 Olympic sailing venue was Weymouth, where sea breezes are common and the wind is typically medium to strong. Since I had only been back training for nine months, I was still really struggling with the physically demanding sheeting in and hiking in a single-handed dinghy like the Laser in strong winds. It was now only six months before the start of the Olympic Games and how well I would perform in the Games was closely linked to how physically strong I could be by then. I didn't even celebrate the Miami World Cup gold medal because I was very aware how little time there was to get fit enough and peak in half a year's time.

As the Miami regatta was mostly in light winds, Jon and I decided to do physical training for the last two days in the United States, while the other team members all went shopping. Even after five days' shopping during the two week stay in Miami, they were still highly enthusiastic and eager to buy more goods that are much cheaper than in China.

This reflects another characteristic of the Chinese – an interest in superficial things rather than deep spiritual values. Most of my teammates would spend all their salaries buying luxury goods, clothing or cosmetics, but grudge paying a penny on any-thing related to sailing. They would spend hours dressing and doing their make-up, or the boys playing games and cards, but refuse to read books or do further study. They would drink excessively and indulge in junk foods while resolving to be healthier and fitter.

Jon used to tease me that the Chinese are scared of everything: the sun (multiple layers of sunscreen and dressed from head to toe), the cold (wearing jumpers, jackets and boots while western-ers are in shorts and sandals) and getting wet (trying to avoid the water when launching), amongst other things.

Normally I would like to tour around whenever I went to a new place. But since the Olympics were getting closer, and my fitness was weak, I wanted to improve my strong wind perfor-mance to be an all-round sailor, consistent in all conditions.

After we hit the road, some light rain appeared. It was not too bad for cycling, and we had been caught in heavy rain quite a few times before and had no problem continuing the training session with a bit more care. However, as I pedalled on a steel bridge, it was so slippery that I fell off my bike with both my palms hitting the ground. All of a sudden my hands were numb and started swelling alarmingly.

Seeing I was in shock, with my hand in an odd position, Jon stopped and came to me: "Don't worry Lily, let's rest for a while before we continue our cycle." He checked that my knees, shoul-ders and wrists were all OK. My bike was absolutely fine as well and he encouraged me to start cycling again. "But I have no feeling in my hands and can't hold the bar at all", I said.

That day Miami was full of police and first aid stations as it was Miami International Marathon day. So we turned to a policeman for some help and he sent me straight to the hospital. After being inspected briefly by an emergency doctor, I was immediately taken for an x-ray. While waiting for the results, Jon called Zulu who was shopping in an outlet store with the rest of the team. Jon reported to the team leader what had happened and asked for my insurance number. Zulu refused to give the number, but offered to drive to the hospital to pick us up as soon as possible.

When the x-ray confirmed that a bone in my left hand was broken, I fainted briefly. The moment I regained consciousness, a group of people were standing around me. Obviously they had discussed something and were arranging to send me back to the hotel to catch the next day's flight back to Shanghai.

This was the first time I had seen Jon extremely angry with a tight black face. It wasn't until I had had my operation in Shanghai that Jon told me the reason why he was so outraged by the team's decision: "everyone in the world goes to Miami for the best hand surgery, but you were flown away from Miami and sent back to China to have the operation. What a stupid action!"

He then added that, if he had known that the team would fly me back to China for the operation, he wouldn't have called the team leader and would have let me have the surgery at once following the American doctor's instruction. Jon did fight hard with Zulu for me to be operated on in Miami, but was stopped physically by a group of Chinese people who screamed in the hospital: "You have no right, Jon! Lily is the property of China!"

Maybe my hand could have had better treatment in the USA, but to some extent the only thought in my mind was whether I would be able to compete in the Olympic Games again. I felt I was being deprived of all my hopes and dreams. Throughout my career I had to fight with numerous injuries and now, six months before the London Olympics, god was once again going to give me a hard time.

The moment I landed in Shanghai, I was driven straight to one of the best hospitals in China. After a series of medical examinations, the operation was planned for early the next morning. My parents were with me that evening and both Zulu and Lima waited outside my hospital room overnight.

Maybe because of his increasing concern, Lima started talking to me again after a long period of silence since the Perth World Championship. This time, however, the team's anger was all directed at Jon, claiming that, if it were not for him, the accident would not have happened. I was then told not to contact Jon anymore and he was not allowed to visit me in hospital. What was more, he was told that I did not want to see him. While the rest of the sailors all went home for an unexpected extra holiday due to the sudden change of plan, Jon was 'confined' securely in the Shanghai Water Sports Centre. We kept talking secretly using SMS, but needed to be very careful not to let anybody see it.

I was treated like a queen: top luxury hospital room, fast track treatment, the best doctors performed the operation and a special diet using imported meat (meat from China tests negative by WADA standards). Even the Shanghai mayor paid a visit, wished me a quick recovery and cheered me up.

After the operation I stayed in Shanghai for another two weeks doing a well-designed and planned recovery programme, while my mum took great care of me. After my stitches were removed, mum accompanied me to Dongshan, Fujian province, the National Sailing Team's training base, for proper physical training while the team doctor did all the treatment for my hand.

In theory I wasn't allowed to sail for three months, which meant that I would miss both the Palma and Hyeres World Cup events. But we decided to go to Hyeres and see how my hand had recovered by then before deciding whether to race or just do some training there.

Although the unlucky accident created a huge obstacle in my Olympic campaign I was not going to allow it to be the end of my world. I had to face it boldly, deal with it positively, and find alternative training methods while not able to sail. I decided to make the most of the situation and focus on improving my core and leg strength as well as endurance, with the goal of getting fitter to hike longer in strong wind.

Jon was banned from seeing me, spending almost a month on his own in China, not allowed to see any sailors or anyone he knew. Despite this he still provided me with the detailed training programme, together with numerous encouraging and positive thoughts: every day I would receive thousands of words in emails on different topics.

I could still do some physical training which wouldn't affect my left hand. I could also use my vivid visualisation technique to replace the actual sailing sessions. I carefully planned my training both in the gym and 'on the water' (actually on a bed) while consulting Jon for his advice.

For fitness I could use the cycling machine and cross trainer to do my aerobics, but not running. I would also do normal leg strength exercises, but upper body work was limited to only those movements which did not use my left hand, which was a bit tricky. I also had to keep my left hand higher than my heart to avoid the swelling increasing.

I remember that the day after my operation I started doing

single leg squats and tummy exercises. On the second day, I walked out of the hospital to try to find a good gym. In China, finding a proper gym is a challenge – even a five star hotel may not have the basic equipment needed. Luckily enough, although there wasn't one within walking distance, there was a fairly professional gym twenty minutes' drive away. From day three after my hand surgery I began the well-planned training routine based around my treatment time.

In the early mornings I took a taxi to the gym to do a strength session; late mornings I met with the doctors for some medical therapy to reduce the swelling and increase the circulation; after lunch I had a rest on my bed while rehearsing my sailing session for about an hour followed by a short nap; late afternoons doing lots of hand recovery exercises with my physio; two hours after an early dinner I headed to the gym again for a longer aerobic session.

Since I was doing aerobics indoors using machines I didn't need to pay close attention like when cycling on a road. So instead of listening to music or watching movies, I devoted all the time doing aerobics to meditating about my sailing. I followed a list of visualisation programmes designed to practise particular basic skills like starting, tacking or rounding marks, racing under all types of wind conditions, correcting my past pitfalls or mistakes and emphasising the key points with self-talks.

By combining the intensity of aerobics with the similarly intensive on the water situations, the visualisation actually helped to push me to reach a higher heart rate and, at the same time, reinforced a precise, positive image about sailing in my subconscious mind. Those mental rehearsals were just like practising for the real life experience and helped me to control the pressure in crucial junctures of the Medal Race or other stressful moments in competition.

When I re-joined the team in Dongshan, Jon and I were prohibited from talking to each other apart from training. Even when doing all those on-land sessions there was always someone spying on us. During that time, my room was just one storey above Jon's. But ironically, despite being so close, we could only communicate by e-mail or text message.

Because of the accident, Jon lost many of his rights as a coach. He was not allowed to decide the training plan or racing schedule and was not allowed to drive the RIB at regattas. Both Zulu and Lima refused everything Jon planned or asked for, and particularly disliked seeing us getting on so well as coach and sailor. In China, the coach's aim is to give their athletes a hard time and they feel superior to the sailors. And the sailors are so afraid of failing to meet the coach's instructions that they barely talk to them. It has been described as a cat and mouse relationship. As a result, sailors rarely share casual conversations with their coaches, and certainly no jokes or laughter. So when Jon and I communicated about training and sailing, we also shared a great number of relaxed conversations and fun experiences. This annoyed the coaches and they limited the time we spent together outside training.

Even the team doctor, Golf, was against Jon, which left me embarrassingly stuck in the middle. On the one hand I wanted to keep a good relationship with the doctor who was spending a huge amount of time on my treatment. On the other hand, Jon couldn't bear that I was still using some old-fashioned healing methods which didn't help my recovery at all.

Here is an example: I was instructed to use heat therapy when my left hand was still swelling several weeks after surgery. The Chinese would only use ice for the first 24 hours and then change to warmth, whatever the situation. Jon strongly recommended to me to stop any heat while I still had swelling, but rather to ice every so often to reduce the swelling and speed my recovery. Culturally, there is a big difference between east and west. In China we always drink hot or warm water and wear a lot to keep warm. Whereas westerners drink iced liquid and wear a lot less than the Chinese when in the same temperature.

Another example was that I was guided to open any wound or minor cut by the Chinese, in order to air the damp area to dry it quicker and heal better. Holding the completely opposite position was Jon who said that I should cover it to avoid it becoming infected and take antibiotics to stop the bacteria spreading.

Once in 2011 I had a small wound on my foot where the toe strap rubbed on my skin. I followed the Chinese doctor's instruction to open and air it and it gradually became more and more infected. Because of this I lost two weeks' sailing and it was not until Jon persuaded me to cover it and use his special 'silver healing' plasters from the UK that it recovered quickly.

In time, Golf was so annoyed that Jon was giving me different ideas, and felt I was doubting and threatening his medical professionalism. Later on, Golf just refused to do any more treatment for some of Jon's shoulder and knee injuries, meaning that Jon had nowhere to turn for sports remedies while coaching in China.

How Jon gradually became disliked by more and more people in the Chinese Sailing Team cannot be covered in a few words. But it was true that many Chinese found him a bit messy and dirty. He would put everything on his bed, even muddy shoes.

He wore ten- to twenty-year-old t-shirts and didn't bother about holes here and there.

In addition, he was so talkative that nobody could stop him. Sometimes, unaware that the Chinese were unwilling to listen, he still went on and on passionately. He would argue fervently to prove a point or persuade someone, which the Chinese leaders and coaches really hated since it meant that they were being questioned or disagreed with.

However, some consideration needs to be made about how hard and demanding Jon's job was while working for the Chinese: he coached the sailors on the water and trained with us in the gym; he had to play games or drink with the coaches and leaders to make them happy so that they would allow us to do what Jon wanted; he also helped team translators to arrange and book all the team's logistics for overseas regattas; and many other things that were outside his coaching role.

He was desperate to get the best possible situation for my campaign, but at the same time was frustrated that many of the team's decisions were actually ruining our plan. Those additional tasks restricted him to a few hours' sleep in the middle of the night. But he always tried to do the most important task and made every minute available for things that would benefit my campaign and didn't mind sacrificing his own personal things.

There were also some culturally related reasons why the Chinese wouldn't recognise him or appreciate his efforts. For example, the British oriented critical thinking approach is very much western, stemming from ancient Greek philosophy: seeking ultimate truth, highly competitive and rigorously defending each argument; whereas the eastern way of thinking comes from Confucian-based philosophy. It strives for peace and harmony, profoundly political, strictly controlled and highly ordered. This explains why questioning or arguing are not rewarded in the east, but criticised and punished. In most western countries, socialising, talking and communicating couldn't be more normal, but that is completely different in China. We should bear in mind those different social perspectives which caused misunderstanding and conflict. Cultural shock or clashes of traditions can cause big problems.

The impenetrable hierarchy grants those leaders the power to decide and choose everything. Coaches are somewhere in the middle and sailors sit with the lowest status. With each level, the lower ones must listen, agree, obey and do whatever the higher one says, commands or asks.

It is this environment and education system that has trained the Chinese to be extremely good at just listening, accepting, copying, following and obeying. They are constantly kept in the dark and blocked by the higher powers. Most people just do as they are told without even a second to think for themselves. You can see that compared to most westerners, the Chinese, and some Asians, are definitely super quiet and do not dare raise their voice in any circumstances.

Interlude 6: Fitness Preparation

Avoiding injuries is the first priority for improving fitness. So make sure that you have a good foundation of a strong core to sustain the intensity and amount of training before undertaking any sports, including a serious (competitive) sailing campaign towards your dream goal. This involves torso stability training to strengthen small muscle groups and joints around your shoulders, lower tummy and gluteus. At the same time it is also important to have a good posture all of the time during your daily life: neck long (feeling tall by imagining a line pulling through the centre of your head), shoulders back and down (imagine pulling your shoulders into your pockets), and tummy in (squeeze the pelvic floor for about 25% all of the time you are awake). These small good habits will benefit your general health throughout your life as well as boosting your ability to perform in sports. Pilates is an extremely valuable exercise system to help protect your spine while maximising flexibility which plays a crucial role in preventing injuries.

Recovery is another issue that has long been under-played. All too often people focus fully on strength and cardio training, but pay no attention to regeneration. The level of recovery is closely linked to the progress of fitness. Physical training is actually a muscle-damaging process; it is only in those periods of rest that you give your body the chance to rebuild itself, making it stronger and tougher after every training session.

Once you realise this simple theory, I believe no one will begrudge giving their body sufficient time to recuperate. What I normally do is always to go for a light cardio session after strong wind sailing, whether it be jogging, running or cross-trainer, followed by a deep relaxing stretch throughout my body. Another one of my favourite routines is doing some self-massage using a foam roller, double balls or massage stick while reading, watching TV or before bed. All of these together cost less than one physio (sports) massage and are easy and light to carry as well!

Chapter 15

The Final Road to Weymouth

I arrived in Hyeres, France, one week before the World Cup event in April 2012. I had started sailing again after two and a half months away from the water. For the first two short sessions my left hand was struggling to grab the mainsheet, and I needed to be ultra-cautious not to bump it on anything. I was risking breaking my hand again if anything unlucky happened, as every steering manoeuvre in the boat was quick, aggressive and abrupt.

My recovering hand just couldn't do it – whenever a movement involved changing hands, I had to wait for my left hand to respond slowly and, at the same time, be careful not to hit anything other than holding the tiller and sheet. Inevitably I was particularly slow during the first few days of sailing and performed like an amateur sailor, especially during starting acceleration, tacking and mark rounding.

To make matters worse, the weather was extremely cold that year, caused by continuous blasts of the Mistral with heavy wind and freezing temperatures. In a few minutes after launching, my hands and feet would go numb, even when I was hiking hard and out of breath. Thinking back, it was pretty dangerous to sail in strong winds with an injured hand, laying myself open to injury if such an accident happened again. By then it would be completely impossible for my left hand to be ready for the Olympics.

However, I was so short of time that I just couldn't allow myself to go into the Games with any regret. I was going to give it all I had. "I am the new Lily, full of good habits. I am going to do my best and really enjoy this event. Every day, and in every way, I am getting better and better. Do little things right and the end results will take care of themselves", I wrote in my diary.

The whole regatta turned out to be the strongest average wind Hyeres has ever experienced. The wind blew hard every day and its speed reached 25-35 knots, with gusts of more than 40. Several times the race management team had to keep us ashore for safety reasons and waited until the wind speed had dropped a bit before sending the sailors out to sea again.

One day it was so windy and wavy that the Race Committee boat could not anchor. I kept on sailing around while Echo just sat in her boat with the sail flapping. Suddenly Lima could not spot her and went into a blind panic. Rather than calmly searching among the fleet he drove about 2-3 nautical miles downwind looking for her. Later the race was postponed and we were sent ashore, happy to find Echo who was just on the far side of the course area.

While ashore, Jon helped me pack up my boat a bit to make sure it wouldn't blow away in the heavy wind. Then he took Echo and me for something to eat while calmly talking about the race without Lima present. I was so relaxed and started to feel a bit sleepy and I went into Jon's van to have a little nap. Jon stayed by the flagpole ready to inform me of any further signals from the race committee.

When the AP (postponement) flag was lowered and the sailors

were released to go afloat, Jon immediately ran to his van, gently woke me and helped me launch. As Lima was nowhere in sight, Jon joined the Israeli coach boat and for the following two races he coached me freely. How nice it was to have my coach in the right place for communication and to get the food or clothing I wanted close to the starting line. I so wished that I could work with Jon one-to-one all the time in the way that we both wanted to.

Much to everyone's surprise, I finished my first regatta after the hand operation with a series win. During the Medal Race my boom hit the water while rounding the bottom mark and I couldn't stop the boat from capsizing (this became the press photo the next day globally!). Jon later explained to me that, instead of fighting with the rudder, what I needed to do in this situation was to just let the tiller go; the boat would then head up by itself and not capsize. However that capsizing totally fired me up and, once my boat was upright, I hiked extremely hard and rolled my biggest rival, Marit, which secured my regatta win. I had never dared to think that my upwind speed could overtake the fastest in the world!

Considering that I hadn't sailed for 75 days, and it was my least favoured strong wind conditions, how did I manage to win this 'mission impossible' regatta? Well, to be honest, the end result was not what I anticipated either, but I knew exactly the reason behind it. Though I was cut off from sailing for months, I was able to concentrate fully on physical training to address my biggest weakness. I did two to four sessions a day, covering strength and aerobics, Pilates and regeneration. I used the fact that I did not need to think about or plan the actual sailing sessions to full advantage. (Normally we aim to make the most of our time on the water and plan our on-land training accordingly to fit in.) I separated my fitness sessions evenly throughout the day to give my body maximum time to recover before undertaking the next one.

For instance, I would train first thing in the morning, and the last session was in the evening. Therefore I could keep pushing myself hard to fulfil the aim of intensive and effective physical training during that particular period of time. Meanwhile I never felt cut off from sailing, as I was meditating for hours, 'steering' my dear Laser dinghy every single day. I set a detailed programme of practice, just as I would have if actually sailing out at sea. I also had the advantage of being able to 'sail' at any time, day or night. Normally I would do a proper racing format during my long aerobic sessions on a stationary bike, and then focus on a specific area which I would most like to improve while lying on a bed before a nap or evening sleep, since those quiet times were fairly short and I often fell asleep not long after my visualisation – I was definitely exhausted after an intensive day, challenged both physically and mentally.

By the time I started sailing again in Hyeres, my fitness had improved considerably, making me no longer vulnerable upwind however strong the wind blew. In the meantime, apart from the limited function in my left hand, my sixth sense of sailing was miraculously preserved after such a long time out of the boat. In reality, I would say that my sailing level had progressed during that non-sailing recovery period, as I successfully cultivated some good racing habits, together with improved steering techniques, by inserting those perfect pictures into my subconscious mind through accumulated mental imagery.

Believe in the power of our brain, it is truly unlimited!

However, despite all the good things about Hyeres, communication between Jon and I became harder. Even though we were staying in caravans next door to each other, most of the communication was by email, with the occasional debrief by the wi fi hotspot at reception.

The team tried to minimise our contact. For example, on my rest day (a Sunday), they took us to Marseille shopping, even though Jon had told them that the shops would be closed. I spent more than half a day in a car for nothing and this really hurt my back which was vulnerable from my lack of pilates. A real waste of a day, but I was delighted to be back in my beloved Laser Radial.

Next up was the World Championship in Germany. One day during racing, Lima drove the RIB onto the course (which coach boats are not allowed to do), despite Jon trying to stop him. This resulted in a protest by the judges, with a serious warning which threatened to add points to my nearest race.

I was leading all the way from day one until the final day of racing. The day before the Medal Race I could not sleep. Rather than just lie on my bed I went downstairs and quietly read my sailing notes. Jon accompanied me, without saying a word, also quietly reading.

On the final day, I correctly spotted that there was more wind pressure on the right while observing the wind before the start. I started at the leeward end, but could not tack onto port, to go right as I wanted, due to a huge pack of boats to windward of me. Watching desperately those boats on the right hand side sailing into huge gusts as the pressure came down, I was unable to cross and reach the favoured area. Those on the right were flat hiking, but those on the left were only sitting on the deck and moving slowly.

Because of my disappointing performance, Lima got so annoyed that he didn't finish watching the final race and drove straight back to the harbour to start packing, leaving all the Chinese girls on the race course area with no food or water. My teammates often cheered for me because my performance would directly affect Lima's mood. Whenever he lost his temper, all the team members would have a hard time, being criticised for everything we did and the cold unpleasant atmosphere would remain for several days or even weeks. What could be happening this time?

The stress from the event, and lack of eating properly, caused me to have a stomach ache while packing the container after the final race. Jon bought me a sandwich and some warm water as soon as he saw something was wrong with me. He quietly talked to me about the race around the container as he knew he would not have the chance to debrief with me face-to-face after the packing work.

The way he talks is always calm and clear which helps me to think and learn from my mistakes, but once Lima starts shouting my mind just can't focus and I am left trembling with fear. Well, Lima saw us talking and immediately assigned Echo, who couldn't speak any English, to work as a pair with Jon. We carried on working separately and, when it came to stack the boats on top of each other, Jon was holding one of the trolley pieces that wouldn't fit.

Lima went into another rage. A few minutes later, when loading another piece of equipment, Jon failed to follow Lima's instructions due to faulty translation by the team translator. Lima got even angrier. The assistant coach physically stopped Lima otherwise it might have led to police involvement.

After the prize giving I was sent straight back to the team house, while every other country's sailors stayed and partied with a free bar. I not only missed all the fun of socialising but had to endure Lima's criticism and punishment.

The last day in Boltenhagen, Germany, Jon and I really wanted to go to the gym as we hadn't been for a long time and gaining fitness was such a key factor for the Olympic Games. However, Zulu and all the other girls wanted to go shopping, so we drove a long time by car to Berlin. Even in the same car, Jon and I 'talked' by text message and we started to plan for the next regatta – Sail for Gold in Weymouth, England.

Another thing which will help you understand more about China is the importance of 'relationship' or 'partnership'. Since the leaders are so powerful, having a good relationship links closely to whether you are allowed to do one thing or another. I am sure those international businessmen who want to succeed in Chinese markets know clearly how the government and leaders can affect their companies. There are also many government firms that completely dominate their specific area since the government has complete control over the laws and manipulates these to make the competitors' business much harder and not give them an equal opportunity.

This will help you understand the following scenario: Jon booked direct flights from Berlin to London with EasyJet, which saved a huge amount of time and money, whereas the Chinese had to fly via Paris with Air China. On this, and so many other occasions, we wasted lots of time by having to use government based businesses wherever possible. What is more, state companies, such as Air China, usually charge twice as much as other 'independent' airlines; for they are the only recognised tickets or invoices that can be used for reimbursement purposes for the Chinese. These little things added together could have made so much difference and enabled us to be fresher for training sooner after a long journey.

The day after we arrived in the UK, Jon's father, Brian, passed away as a result of Motor Neurone disease, during which people could hardly understand his words. Jon knew it might happen any day during the Worlds, but kept it to himself. He knew that his strong emotions could have affected my mood and distracted me from racing.

He literally ran after landing in London to try to see his dad one last time. Brian must have waited for Jon before saying goodbye to this world. Earlier Jon had mentioned my name to his father a few times and all his family knew he was coaching the Chinese team at that time. One of Jon's last sentences to his father was: "I love you very much but I just have to go and help the little Chinese girl now". Brian replied enthusiastically, but Jon couldn't understand his exact words. Jon just wished his dad could have lived to see Lily's gold medal.

Jon returned to the team and was back on the water the day after scattering his father's ashes on the farm where he grew up. Now it was time to focus on Weymouth, not just for the World Cup event but, more importantly, as the Olympic venue. However, the RIB tricks by Lima continued:

Day 1: Jon helped me to launch and when he went to the RIB, Lima had gone without Jon. Jon then jumped into the Swedish coach's boat which was just leaving and asked him to drive to Lima quickly. Jon managed to jump in before Lima could stop him.

Day 2: Jon helped me launch and he ran to the RIB, but they had gone already (again!). This time he jumped in with Ben Paton from England who was coaching the girl from Cook Island. Jon put my stuff in Lima's RIB, but when he tried to get on board with Lima, Lima drove away quickly. Jon just stayed with Ben for that day's racing.

Day 3: Jon helped me launch and calmly walked to Ben and they towed out Ben's sailor at the same time as Lima towed me out. When they arrived, Lima rammed Ben's RIB and the Chinese assistant coach snatched my bag before driving away.

Day 4 onwards: Ben's girl was in the silver fleet, so Jon had Ben's RIB all to himself. We worked and communicated together so well, and I learnt about wind bends, current and got more familiar with the Olympic venue. In addition, Jon would take videos while on the water and talk as he shot, so that I could have it as part of our debrief since it was impossible to analyse the video together and talk to me directly once coming ashore.

In the Medal Race, Lima again sat on the course at the windward mark most of the time. His boat was so obvious – it was bright yellow. Jon had to work very hard to stop others from protesting him.

Lima's temper could be terrible. When he shouted at me I found I would forget everything and struggle to focus. After going from 1st to 4th overall in the Medal Race, as I misjudged the starboard lay line and had to gybe round, I knew that soon after I'd finished I would have to face Lima's rage. However Jon was prepared this time: he came to me first in his RIB and pretended to shout and scream at me (something he would never do). He did it with a wink and a smile on his face, but Lima never knew. So Lima didn't bother to punish me as he thought Jon already had. Indeed both Lima and Zulu were delighted, thinking that Jon and I were no longer getting on so well.

There has always been so much stress in the team, and Jon did his utmost to keep me happy. One time he arranged for me to have a secret dinner with my Pilates instructor Jenny Glover. As soon as we finished the Pilates session that day, Jon bought food and drink in the nearest pub. At first he had joined us, but later made an excuse and left Jenny and me to have a lovely girls' chat.

Jenny actually came down to see me in the Weymouth and Portland Sailing Academy during Sail for Gold and was completely shocked when she saw Lima shouting at Jon.

Jon also created some fun activities for Echo, like doing Taekwondo, but had kept this secret as well. Unfortunately the translator told Golf in a casual chat and Lima heard about it and warned Echo never to do it again. Jon also took Echo for a KFC meal afterwards. Jon hates junk food, but he knew it was something that Echo would enjoy and he wanted to make her happy and motivated as well.

The situation with Jon was getting worse and worse. He was not only denied driving a RIB to coach me (even though there was another RIB in our container in good condition which Lima didn't allow him to use), sometimes Lima just drove off without him. On some occasions, Jon would go on some other coach's boat and never bother to try to get on Lima's RIB. He could then position himself to watch my racing clearly, whereas Lima normally sat far behind the starting line and rarely moved as the race went on. For me, it was also much more pleasant as I could then talk to Jon freely, without worrying about anything that might annoy Lima. Also I would have my waterproof jacket as soon as I finished racing to keep myself warm until the last minute before the next preparatory signal.

Jon and I were not allowed to talk apart from while training or racing. In those days I dreamt of having a little walk and easy relaxing talk with Jon after dinner. Even though we lived almost next to each other in the caravan park (I shared one caravan with female teammates and Jon shared one with Lima and Zulu), we communicated mostly through e-mails and text messages.

Occasionally we would meet and have a quick chat about that day's training by the reception early in the morning when everyone else was still fast asleep, and walked separately to and from the caravans to avoid bumping into anyone accidentally. Too often Jon had so much to say to me, but had to squeeze it into a few minutes, or sometimes a few seconds on the water while on Lima's RIB.

Later on, Jon designed a few key words to help me remember the most important things, such as: the three Cs: consistent, conservative, controlled aggression; pressure is king; big roll tack; keep centralising; get my head out of the boat; bow down in the short chop; this is my day; go on Lily, go for it; and so on.

He would always help me to rig, launch, de-rig the boat and use those precious moments to talk to me briefly. We managed to do our debrief while doing aerobics training together. After my bike incident in Miami, I was forbidden to do any more road cycling, only indoor bikes. So Jon and I utilised all our time on a cross trainer or stationary bike to have our little sailing talks. But there were still times when we failed to play the game well enough and I couldn't completely hide from the other Chinese

141

my enjoyment while working with Jon. Unfortunately this led to an even deeper rage from Lima who sometimes couldn't control his anger and shouted at me many times in public.

As a Chinese, this kind of behaviour was not terribly alarming and I had been brought up experiencing criticism and physical punishments. But I was still amazed when Lima was even more outrageous and kicked or sometimes hit Jon. I could hardly imagine what this meant to a westerner, and especially a polite, civilised Englishman whose only aim was trying to help me. My utmost respect goes to Jon as he just walked away quietly and didn't fall into the trap of what might well have been some serious physical fighting.

Lima was envious of Jon's capability as a coach and was feeling threatened by an 'outsider' who had worked with me for just one year, while he had been in the team for decades. But this still couldn't justify treating a foreign coach as he pleased following the Chinese tradition and style. The way he thought and behaved makes me feel ashamed of my nation when revealing it here.

Many of you might say: couldn't you choose your own coach? Unfortunately, no. Because of the hierarchies in China, coaches are well above the sailors, so they have the sole right to choose who can be in the team. If it were not for the fact that I was then the best sailor in China, I would have been kicked out of the team years ago. For a long time, I had been regarded as an alien by many Chinese because I thought and acted differently to others, leaving me very unpopular among certain groups of people. Coaches hated me for not listening to everything they said; my parents criticised me for not being a 'good girl' or behaving in a way that they hoped; sailors disliked me for doing extra training by myself; leaders blamed me when I questioned their ideas.

Even the diet I had as a professional athlete would repel most Chinese. They would not accept that the food I ate could provide more energy and boost my performance when they firmly believed that meat was the only engine for athletes. So no wonder that they would keep on telling the sailors to have more pork, beef or chicken. Furthermore, the Chinese are big fans of deep fried food, oily cuisines, and love to consume lots of feet, skin and fatty pieces of different animals, which is the least helpful to athletes. The chef in the team would cook three to five different kinds of meat in every meal, with only white rice as a source of carbohydrate.

All in all, people in every part of my life found me strange enough. I accepted being labelled as 'mad', but just took it lightly and forgot about it. For I have beliefs in what I do. I have reasons why I choose to deal with things in a certain way, and I was determined to turn my goals into reality on the road to fulfil my dreams.

However, when Jon came into my sailing career, it gradually changed my self-image. Not only did he help me to build my self-confidence, but he also convinced me that I was not doing something 'wrong'. It was actually those who chose to lead an easy and secured life, to just believe what they had been told and to do as they had been ordered, who were 'crazy'. My life suddenly lit up after sharing so many common thoughts, habits and beliefs with Jon. I was no longer feeling lonely in this world, and we enjoyed so many wonderful talks, a positive atmosphere, healthy foods and scenic journeys. (Thank god I am not an alien!)

Jon's attitude to training was also new to me. As you will know by now, the Chinese approach is to train, train and train, with no time off, like battery hens in a cage, just producing the (hopefully golden) eggs. Jon knew it was a balance between training, rest and nutrition, and he also made training enjoyable as well as productive.

On one occasion in Weymouth, I was just too exhausted to train. Jon knew something was wrong as I always trained hard and never gave up. He took me to the pub just next to the gym and I had the chance to recover, and a welcome bit of freedom. We didn't switch off completely, we talked about yellow flags (for propelling the boat illegally), being penalised as a premature starter and the balance between too much risk and not enough. So it wasn't time wasted, but most importantly it meant I was fresh enough the next day to have a good sailing session.

That year Jon gave me a book called *Wild Swans*, which was written by a Chinese writer, Jung Chang, who later married an Englishman. It was a good book which reflected the Chinese history, culture and hierarchy in the story of three women in different generations of the same family. The author was the youngest, who was born in 1952, and subsequently became the first Chinese to obtain a PhD degree in a British University in Linguistics. Her family background, which covered the whole period of the Civil War as well as the Cultural Revolution during 1967-77, was completely in contrast to her later life in the UK.

She tells the true story from the end of the 19th century and her grandmother's situation during Empire China, to her mother's fatal experience around the severe war period in the mid-20th century, all the way until the end of the Cultural Revolution, where she herself suffered terribly. It revealed not only the recent history of China, but also culture-related topics such as people's way of thinking, including their beliefs and religion, inequality issues, human rights, the governing body, lifestyle and media bias. She then compared these aspects with her western life having studied at York University and married the Englishman, Jon Halliday.

As she put it in her book: "Britain was a marvellously classless society. I was born into the Communist elite and saw how class-ridden and hierarchical Mao's China was. Everyone was slotted into a rigid category... 'date of birth', 'sex', 'family background'... These determined one's career, relationships and life... But meeting people in London, I sensed none of these pressures. Everyone seemed to be extraordinarily equal, and could not care less about backgrounds".

I couldn't agree with her more since I have started studying at university in the UK myself now. It helps me understand more about the western and eastern societies and further opened my eyes about my country and helped me understand why people are so different. But the sad fact is that her book is still banned in China, a decade after its first publication, despite having sold more than 13 million copies and having become one of the best-selling books in the world, translated into 37 languages so far. This confirms Jung's remark of a 'deadly controlled country' which refuses to be honest with the past.

Positive Affirmation 7: Strong Tummy

I have a very strong tummy to support my lower back. I pull my tummy in from the time I wake to the time I sleep. I zip up and hollow while doing Pilates to strengthen the core muscles. I use neutral or lateral breathing which encourages correct movement patterns by enabling me to stay centred while I move. I put my shoulders back and down to have a good posture.

I do some visualisation to help communication between my brain and the muscles. I make sure that my tummy is in all the time and think of the spine being long and wide. I keep good posture all the time: stand tall, sit high, shoulders and chin down, knees forward, lift ribs from hips. I gain a greater feeling of working all the muscles, especially the un-used, smaller ones, by elongating through the whole movement.

I develop a thinking body, with complete mental control over all the muscles to synchronise my stable, precise movement and open, natural breathing. While sitting or standing I engage the b-line core like a rod; keep the ribs lengthened away from the hips at the sides; press the shoulder blades toward the tailbone; lengthen through the crown of the head. When in a supine position, I bend my knees or hold my legs in the air rather than extended on the ground. I have calmer breathing, a flatter back, and less facial expression, my exercises look very easy.

I rehearse this positive affirmation daily.

Chapter 16

Olympic Glory

In the first chapter I told you about sailing in the London 2012 Olympic Games and winning the Medal Race and gold medal.

The prize giving ceremony was due to begin at 6pm on the Medal Race day. It was held right by the slipway where the boats launch with the huge five-colour Olympic ring statue above the water. Since all the spectators were on the Nothe Hill, and not allowed to enter the Olympic sailing venue, the ceremony was mainly watched by team members, supporters and journalists from different countries around the world. The then ISAF Vice-President, Teo Ping Low, presented the medals for the Women's single-handed dinghy: the Laser Radial class.

The skin all over my body always goes funny whenever the Chinese national anthem is played, and it did so again in that special moment on what might be the biggest and most memorable day of my life. Singing the national song evoked my full patriotism and sense of pride in what I had achieved in the highest competition in sport.

My mind played 'movies' by itself, going through all the sorrows and bitterness as well as the happiness and excitement of the whole journey. I was content, not merely because I had won an Olympic gold medal, but also because of all the progress I had made alongside my sailing career. I knew I had tried my utmost and done my very best, leaving no regret for the rest of my life, which is undoubtedly the greatest spiritual treasure.

I travelled to London and spent the next few days doing numerous interviews and photoshoots. Because I had to talk endlessly in front of all the media, my throat was constantly sore. After only a few days away from sailing, I missed it terribly: the freedom, the joy, the closeness to nature.

On the morning of the Closing Ceremony, I received the very short notice that I had been selected to carry the national flag for my country. Before that, there were lots of rumours about this or that athlete being the flag-bearer, and all the Chinese people were guessing who would be the lucky one. The main focus was, of course, on the popular Chinese sports such as table tennis, diving or badminton.

When it was officially announced that I would be carrying the flag, it was a great surprise because very few people in China know about the sport of sailing. It was said that my personal story and spirit of conquering all the barriers and setbacks touched many people and they wanted me to be a role model for all the young Chinese, inspiring them to chase their dreams boldly and optimistically. It was such a huge honour and I had never dared think of being a flag-bearer at the Olympic Ceremony.

Among the 204 nations, several other sailors were selected to carry their national flag: Ben Ainslie for Great Britain; Malcolm Page for Australia; Allan Norregaard for Denmark; Colin Cheng for Singapore; Alejandro Foglia Costa for Uruguay; Fredrik Loof for Sweden and Damien Desprat for Monaco.

All the flag-bearers marched into the stadium together, while thousands of team members from the 28 different sports were already waiting at the designated area. It was rather like a massive music festival, with everyone singing world famous songs together: from classical to rock, country to folk, jazz to pop. What a magnificent scene and thrilling experience!

Chapter 17

Heat after London

"You've got to deal with the post-Olympic heat for a whole year", a former Olympic Champion said to me after I had won the Games in London 2012.

Living in the limelight is not as superb as you might think: talking with the media for hours, signing autographs for thousands, standing still and smiling with unceasing camera flashes are just a small part of being a celebrity.

I used to hope that, if I won an Olympic gold medal for my country, the world would only know that there was a Chinese girl taking the title, without knowing who she was. I naively wished that I could keep my ordinary life and not lose my privacy.

I must admit that I did not enjoy the 'Olympic Champion' lifestyle because in the months that followed, my body was under a lot of stress from the ever-increasing demands put on it from all areas of society: my eyes were terribly red, my throat was extremely sore, I was deprived of sleep and always on the move, flying once or twice every day!

But despite this, I am extremely grateful for all the support I was given in my sailing career and I want to give this back to my country. I think I have a golden opportunity to promote sailing in China. So, however unpleasant or boring these public activities or hospitality appearances were to me, I always acted in the best way I could. I showed my passion for sailing, shared my inspirational stories and enthusiastically accepted as many requests as I could and tried to help lots of charitable organisations.

I also had the opportunity to meet and talk with many elite professionals and specialists in different careers and learnt something unique directly from them, which would never have been possible without becoming an Olympic Champion. It truly opened many doors for me to interact with those excellent people and broadened my experience as a young person, which I will never forget.

It also brought me some fabulous memories. Winning the 2012 ISAF Rolex World Sailor of the Year Awards in Dublin, Ireland, was second to none. However, even that gave me some challenges. As I had never worn an evening dress before, I had no idea where to buy one. In China, wearing formal dresses is not common and most people would never have one in their entire life. However, it seems that such a dress code is used for many occasions in western societies: attending a wedding reception, big parties and formal dinners.

I was rather concerned in preparing for that special evening in Ireland. I searched and walked through the whole city centre in Shanghai, but didn't find a single shop selling that type of dress. Perhaps I am an unfashionable girl and just didn't know the right place to buy one. It is true: I rarely dress up or put on make-up. I always hit the book stores when my female friends go shopping. Every evening when they are putting on face masks, or spending hours doing their make-up, I just indulge in my own study and read books. It is not just that I am a diligent learner, or have strong self-discipline, I simply find the world of knowledge much more attractive than superficial beauty.

In the end, I hired a dress from a wedding photography shop. (Such a shop will also be a funny concept to you westerners. The Chinese often spend thousands of pounds taking perfect wedding photographs before sending out the wedding invitations to their family and friends. They then have many different photos, with various dresses and backgrounds, to decorate the wedding ceremony, which makes the whole experience truly unique and very special for the newlyweds.)

The nominees for the ISAF Rolex Female World Sailor of the Year were:

- Tamara Echegoyen, Angela Pumariega & Sofia Toro (ESP), who won gold in the Women's Match Racing at the London 2012 Olympic Games
- Helena Lucas (GBR), who won gold in the 2.4mR class at the London 2012 Paralympic Games
- Saskia Sills (GBR), who won windsurfing gold in the 2012 ISAF World Youth Sailing Championship
- Lijia Xu (CHN)

Even though none of us would know who the winner was until the final second when His Majesty, King Constantine of Greece, announced it, I still wrote out a short speech in the hope that I could share my little story with the whole sailing world. Thanks to my preparation in advance, the speech turned out to be a great success. It was genuine, inspirational and touched almost everyone in the room. Here is the full speech if you missed it:

"There was a time that I complained that god was unfair to me for I share

only half of the listening ability of ordinary people. There was a time when I complained that god was unfair to me for my left eye can barely make out any character. And there were times when I faced retirement due to my hand and leg surgery, as well as some other severe injuries. However I am lucky enough to have been able to continue sailing to this day and conquered all the difficulties and setbacks that confronted me. Looking back, all those mentioned were merely testing elements and processes god was using to try to figure out whether I was worthy of becoming an Olympic Champion.

Sailing gives me the opportunities to chase my dreams; sailing presents me the stage to show my potential; sailing provides me the capacity to see, feel and explore the world; and sailing leads me to a path of a better life — a life full of vitality, excitement and joyous experiences.

Nowadays I've learnt to cherish every square inch of my body and be grateful for all it can do and how it supports me. Life is full of happiness when I truly open my eyes with a positive attitude and embrace it, appreciate it with my whole, genuine, loving heart.

Thank god for sailing! What a life-long sport!"

In early 2013 I also won the highest sports award in China and attended the CCTV (China Central television) ceremony in Beijing. Again I prepared a little poem for my speech which impressed the Chinese audience. I am a big fan of literature and becoming a freelance writer is part of my dream.

Although sailing isn't as popular as some other sports in China, that evening put all the focus on me and sailing. All of a sudden, millions of tweets were talking about me, and I was at the top of the news in numerous media the following day. I surely became the most glittering sports star from that award ceremony. To give you a little taste of what I said, let me translate the rough meaning of the little poem into English:

"Whether I win or lose, my support team is always there; no regret, no complaint.

Whether I am happy or sad, my friends are always there; no sorrow, no tear.

Whether I am healthy or injured, my parents are always there; no retreat, no withdrawal.

Thank you all who cultivated today's Lily.

I hope I can make Chinese sailing famous in the world like when Zhen He first sailed round the world 600 years ago.

Whether you are men or women, young or old, tall or short, rich or average, sailing is always there, waiting for you to explore.

A healthy, free, stylish and environmentally friendly sport.

Let's carry all our dreams on a sailboat and discover the beauty of this world."

Positive Affirmation 8: Elegance is an Attitude

I am an elegant, healthy girl who treats herself with love, care and respect. I am blessed to have people's love, and cherish every possible contact with my truly loved ones. I am keen to learn new things and work hard to improve myself. I am enthusiastic about helping others and excel in my career.

By prioritising the things that I need to do daily beforehand, I manage my schedule wisely and also take time off occasionally. I exercise every day to keep fit, and eat healthy food to nourish my body. I can control my life rationally, achieving a good balance between family, career and a social life.

I listen to my body and eat natural food in the right portions according to my needs. By reducing the amount I eat at every meal I give my stomach more freedom and comfort. I pay special attention while travelling and switch the desire to eat to acquiring knowledge by reading, writing, or watching movies.

I get up slowly after lying down to give my blood pressure time to rise; I take time to eat and enjoy tasty food, and value the chance to communicate with family or friends; I step and move lightly to reduce any noise and I am patient in using everything little by little and truly enjoy their benefit.

I do every simple thing with wisdom and control. My aim is to be a good citizen for every society and be environmentally friendly.

Grace in everything.

Chapter 18

Thoughts about China

As a communist country, China is a one-party nation. Every Chinese dreams of becoming a member of the party, but only the elite among the elite have the opportunity. One of the biggest motivations is that a party member has a far better chance to obtain a good job, and party members are the most likely to get a promotion later on.

While this doesn't particularly attract me, the day I turned 18 years old, both my parents and leaders urged me to apply to join the Communist Party. The same practice of writing an application has continued for decades: demonstrating how good the party is; how it leads to public prosperity; how I am going to work hard and win glory for the nation; how much I am prepared to sacrifice in my own life whenever my country needs me; swearing to serve all the Chinese people with enthusiasm; and obey any order the party asks me to do.

However, even though millions write these applications and submit them to the senior leaders, only hundreds are accepted as party members. It was only after I had won three World Championships and one Olympic medal that I was finally approved as a member of the party.

My parents were so happy that they immediately told all their relatives and friends, which I guess earned them lots of kudos and showed how proud they were of their daughter joining the dominant Communist Party.

Nevertheless, I was not a well-behaved party member as I didn't listen to some of my leaders' instructions, nor did I obey all of their commands, which put me in a difficult position and they threatened to punish or expel me from the party. I have utmost understanding and respect for my country, but I desire more freedom to do things I want to do instead of following someone else's ideas. Maybe I am not very Chinese in some ways…

*

Every year when I go back home to Shanghai, I cannot recognise some areas because of the huge changes and development all over the city: numerous skyscrapers here and there; a few more underground lines; several viaducts rising up overhead; taxis and buses upgraded all the time; numerous blocks of apartments in both the city and rural districts accompanied by massive shopping malls for those communities.

China is truly the fastest growing country in the world, but there are also some downsides: more cars causing more traffic; millions of people from the countryside moving into the cities causing overcrowding; uncontrolled industrialisation contributing to serious air pollution; high inflation pushing house prices up astronomically; and so on. These are the sacrifices that every Chinese has to pay for the economic advances.

However there have been benefits. My family's position has improved dramatically: from my grandparents who lived in poverty; to my parents with limited food coupons to feed themselves; to five family members sharing a 20 square metre flat; to 2009 when I bought my first three-bedroom flat, with my own room and bed for the first time in my entire life, with lack of food no longer being an issue. How lucky my generation is to have so many new opportunities and to benefit from what has been accumulated by several generations before us.

But, as you will have realised in reading this book, China is not just about the party and economic development – there are some cultural differences which may surprise you.

*

There was an unwritten rule in the Sailing Team that women could have three days' rest when they had their period every month. From the Chinese perspective, women cannot do any physical activities during menstruation as it will be very harmful to their body and increases the risk of infection if female sailors were exposed to sea water. So coaches and sailors agreed to have three days off from any physical training and sailing during their period.

This didn't strike me as odd until I started working with some of the foreign coaches who could not understand it. To not train for three days in a row would affect training progress and result in 36 days lost training a year! And we would have to race anyway if our period came during a regatta.

I hold a neutral position on this, as I partially agree with both sides. On the one hand, I do feel the need for a rest when menstruating as I personally experience lots of pain in my tummy and feel very weak. On the other hand, I've got used to it and learnt to deal with the same situation that every female sailor encounters at several events every year.

So what I do is to keep up some physical training, but reduce the total amount and intensity. For example, I can still do upper and lower body strength, but probably not core as it triggers my painful tummy. I can also do some light to medium aerobics in order to retain my endurance level. At least I can maintain my fitness, without any loss, by doing some training during my period – far better than stopping for three days and re-starting again, taking more time to regain the normal fitness level. If a regatta unfortunately clashed with my period, then I had to take painkillers to keep my focus on track.

When I talked to several foreign female sailors, they were all surprised to learn that the Chinese team had this special 'privilege' for women. It never occurred to them to have a rest when they had their period and it didn't seem to have any negative effect on them.

Are there really some genetic differences between western and eastern people? Only scientists can tell, but there is a colourful saying very popular among the Chinese which has some relation to this topic: "The westerners won't feel cold because they eat butter and cheese for breakfast whereas the Chinese have white rice porridge and so do not have enough calories to give sufficient energy out nor the fat to keep the body warm".

It seems true that the Chinese need to wear a lot more clothing compared to westerners under the same climatic conditions. It is also true that there is quite a lot of difference in the calories and energy from these two kinds of breakfast. But this is just an entertaining discussion topic for you, and certainly not a sound argument – I hope you enjoyed it and didn't smile too smugly!

Another consequence of the Chinese Team's rules is perhaps more serious. As I have already told you, we were encouraged not to be feminine and not allowed to have a love affair before the age of 25. Possibly as a result, some of my female teammates became lesbians. Being intimate with their girlfriends would not attract much suspicion from the coaches, since girls holding hands and sharing a bed are quite common in China. There was also much less chance of them being punished or dismissed for having a secret relationship with their same-sex mates than having a boyfriend, which was forbidden.

However, same-sex marriage is not legalised in China, and a long way from being recognised or understood by Chinese people or society as a whole. As a result my teammates are in endless secret relationships. Some were even prepared to marry a man so that they wouldn't be despised or judged negatively by people around them, while keeping secret their affairs with their girlfriends.

Chapter 19

My Puppy Love

This is probably the right time to tell you about my love experiences.

Not long after the Beijing Olympics in 2008, I went to Shanghai Jiaotong University to do my undergraduate study. At the same time I was being treated for several injuries. I really enjoyed the peaceful life of study and indulged myself in the world of knowledge and being in the midst of open, genuine and smart people. There was also a lot more freedom in the university and much less control compared with the atmosphere in the sailing team. Probably because of this I fell in love for the first time at the age of 23.

I remember when I first chatted with Paige Railey (USA Radial sailor) in Busan in 2005 and she was astonished to hear that I didn't know what a couple's kiss felt like, since Chinese sailors were not allowed to have a relationship until their mid-twenties. I guess it sounds ridiculous to you westerners and maybe you would react in the same way that Paige did.

For the first time, I would like to reveal my private diary and share my experience of that first relationship. From it you will see the different perspective of love and marriage between the east and the west. When I look through my diary now I cringe a bit, seeing myself as a little pristine and naive, but it clearly reflects the deeply rooted culture and ways of thinking in China.

I am also amazed how much I've changed since living in the UK and really pleased that I have escaped from those stereotypical and superficial beliefs. Before I came abroad I never believed there were true love relationships as I grew up in an environment full of fighting couples and broken marriages. I never saw my parents having any intimacy between them: no kissing, no hugging, no holding hands, and no mention of sweet words like "I love you".

In contrast, whenever I travelled to western countries, there was no shortage of couples holding hands on the street and being affectionate towards each other. Moreover I feel that family is the most crucial part in western societies whereas career, money and face were the priorities for Chinese people.

My parents arranged many blind dates when some friends introduced rich and powerful men from a decent family background. They felt my whole life would be secured by marrying such a man with a good career and expensive properties. In this respect I never acted as a 'good girl' and refused to accept their 'commands'. Later, it was those western couples truly loving each other and prioritising their family life that gradually convinced me of the existence of true love in this world.

So here are some extracts from my private diary:

1: Mr. Right

Walter: he is not handsome but charming; he is not a genius but knowledge-able; he is not romantic but modest; he is not talkative but affectionate; he is not tall but at least as tall as me; he is not strong but knows how to take care of me; he is not rich but a smart and hard worker...... From the moment I met him, I knew I belonged to him.

It is quite hard to believe that we two have so many habits and interests in common. What is more, some of my characteristics which used to be considered negative turned out to be positives to him. How can you find a mate who treasures you so much? I have nothing more to ask for.

2: *Love Descended On Me*
Dear Walter,

I have so many feelings inside my heart after seeing you last night. Lying on my bed for a couple of hours, I couldn't get to sleep. I don't know how I finally managed to fall asleep but then only to find myself awake at 5 o'clock this morning. I have never had this kind of feeling before – heart beating, nervous and excited, and I couldn't stop thinking about you all day. I didn't believe in 'love at first sight' before, and didn't expect that it would actually happen to me! You are almost my perfect 'Mr. Right', but I know that you won't have such strong feelings as me, because I have never experienced this before.

Remember when you asked me whether I was trying to find my soulmate for the purpose of marriage or was just looking for fun, and I didn't reply to you? Now I'd like to explain the main reason: we are both not casual people and I know you have no time to waste on any love relationship without marriage. The first thought in my mind after you asked was that I was frightened of hurting you.

As we both know, the moment I go back to the sailing team, it will be really difficult for us to maintain our relationship and I have seen too many couples breaking up because of their distance apart. It's too challenging for you to wait for me for another few years and I will feel guilty about that, too. I hope you can lead a happy and healthy life if you can find someone else better than me, or at least someone who can be with you most of the time.

You know what is in my mind now? I outlined a dream future life which is to work at the University Sports Centre so that we can live together near your workplace. We go out to the countryside at the weekends and travel around China or abroad in our school holidays. I am more than happy to help you lead a healthy life including adequate exercise and nutritional diet.

If, for instance, I was already retired from my sports career now, it might be easier for us to be lovers. But I am very sorry to say that sailing is a must-do for me. Without it, my life would become meaningless. Though I know how demanding it is to get to the top, I am willing to sacrifice something in seeking my life's true value. The end might not be good or worthy, but at least I won't have any regret when I get old.

So my position is quite clear to you now, it is your turn to make the decision. Do you want to take the risk to be my other half? Or will you stick to your original plan for life?

Sincerely,

Lily

3: Lily's Puppy Love

At the age of 23, I finally begin my first love. Too late? I used to think so, but now I am contented. As a matter of fact I have to admit that having a love affair can really be a distracting factor: no wonder those who fall in love can no longer concentrate on their study or work, especially when you are alone or before sleep. Insomnia is a must-learn-to-deal-with situation when you begin or finish a love affair. I've already experienced the former for three nights in a row, hopefully I don't need to experience the latter...

He said that he was nervous about our first meeting, to which I replied to him that I was the opposite: I was quite calm that day, but my heart has beaten twice as fast as normal from the night after we met. The next time we saw each other, instead of hearing the words "will you be my girlfriend?" or something like that which I hoped he would ask, he just immediately held my hand without any warning while we were wandering around the school campus. I was a little embarrassed as I hadn't prepared for that at all, but who cares! Just want to enjoy that precious moment...

4: Our Parents

Honey, first of all I want to apologise for having caused so much trouble to you yesterday, driving around and waiting so long, which prevented your parents from having dinner at the usual time. So from now on please promise to me not to carry all these burdens of life on your shoulders as you are no longer single by yourself. I'm part of your life, your soul, your support. I'll be much happier to share your joys and sorrows, and also some responsibilities, rather than letting you undertake all those tasks alone. Please don't hesitate to ask me when you need any help or to tell me if there's anything I can do to assist you in order to reach our mutual goal. Mention one case when I can go somewhere by myself instead of waiting for you to pick me up. You don't need to take me everywhere simply because you possess a car.

Well, to get back to the point, what I want to convey is: please don't treat me like a princess. I know that you want to protect me, take care of me, or accompany me, but you mustn't make your lover worry more about you while unable to do anything for you. So again, don't keep doing everything alone as I am one of your hands – your darling girlfriend!

Ok, the topic is about our parents. I used to think that meeting the elderly was just to respect them: being polite, showing affection and caring about them. I like talking and chatting with them and so I was perfectly happy to meet your parents yesterday as well. It was only then that I realised that meeting one's lover's parents is quite the opposite. It's kind of like an examination and they are the examiners. The conversation was mainly about introducing me, in much more detail than on any other occasion. And your parents did not make even a minimal effort to hide their curiosity about my personal life which made me a little uncomfortable.

Now I began to understand that most parents will ask in the same way, because my parents behaved very much like yours when I mentioned you to them when we met the first time. Their only purpose is wanting their child to have a blissful marriage, establish a suitable family and lead a happy life. So hopefully next time when you have the chance to visit my home and meet my parents, they won't be too hard on you. But being prepared is always the best policy!

5: *Our Fifth Date*
A traditional dinner at a western restaurant with a tranquil, romantic, and exotic environment.

An American movie, Wall Street: Money Never Sleeps, showed the character for each of us. The main couple is just like us: you are a stock speculator, and I am an incorruptible person. Is it just another coincidence or a prelude of our future?

We both have a strong sense of desire to prove our special ability in our beloved 'job' or 'interest' – me in sailing, you on the stock market, both searching for a way to realise our brilliant, meaningful or successful careers. But deep in our hearts, we still dream of having a normal family and an ordinary life. So if, one day, we do achieve our goals, let's not forget to remind each other of our true nature as human beings; not to lose the most significant values of life: money isn't everything, the most precious gift is happiness within, inside our heart, our mind and our soul.

Well, the good thing is that we are progressing quite smoothly, aren't we? With me, you start to travel by public transport instead of driving a private car; with you, I experience my first loving relationship; with us, we try our utmost to improve our personalities in order to match the other half even better. Those bad habits or ideas which had taken root in either of us for years, we are now starting to change consciously and willingly.

Thousands of words spoken by the parents don't match a lover's single word. And maybe that is the power that love has. One day we might have nothing more to talk about, or one day we might not appeal to the other half any longer. But I still want to accompany you: lying beside you, hearing your breath, listening to your heartbeat, feeling the warmth or your body...

That is all I wish for; I am longing just to be with you in a long and peaceful life.

6: Can't Wait To See You

A week has gone by before I am finally able to sit down and write something here after getting rid of those heavy school assignments.

Firstly, to my dear dad, how grateful I am for inviting us to dinner the other day - you couldn't imagine. I could see the pure emotion of how concerned parents are about their child's future life and marriage. I was deeply touched by what you said to Walter and also more than grateful for your most sincere and earnest talk which was like a father-son conversation with him.

And for you, Walter, if there was anything about what my father said, his sentences or behaviour, that insulted you, please don't mind and don't take it to heart. As it had already been made quite clear to you, he is a direct, wildly-gesticulating, loud-speaking man with poor Mandarin. (Walter is from Zhejiang Province so he cannot understand Shanghainese). But he is also a down-to-earth, approachable and easy-going people-person. He may be conceited, ill-mannered, and presumptuous, but he never ceases to be a loving, hospitable, and kind-hearted father or friend.

Since you two now know each other to some extent, you can talk to him directly any time. I am sure that, little by little, your honesty, your intelligence and your sincerity will all be recognised, until one day both my dad and mum are aware of and touched by your personality. It is not what you buy them that matters, but the communication and understanding.

I will be fervently looking forward to seeing our parents meet together one day in the near future: dads having a drink, mums gossiping about us, and what we two need to do is only to take care of them and make them happy

167

& at ease. And the most significant one: to convince them that we will be a suitable couple who will address their worries about our future and life. What a beautiful scene, isn't it?

The End

Not long after I went back to the team, Walter and I calmly broke up because we couldn't see each other and his parents pressed him to get married within a year since he was already over 30. It seems as if marriage is a chore for the Chinese and you will be despised or judged by people if you are still single after 30. A woman aged over 27 is called a 'left-over woman' and is deemed to be not doing her duty of being a wife and mother or is seen as having trouble finding a partner. However, considering it was not long ago that arranged marriage was the norm in the east, having the freedom to choose your own partner is already a bonus!

Chapter 20

A New Path

After the London Olympic Games, my desire to study over-
powered the motivation of doing another four-year Olympic
campaign. Over the previous 16 years my whole life had been
wholly devoted to sailing and, especially as a Chinese athlete, I
had no freedom to experience things other than sailing. I felt I
had missed so many amazing things and places in life and was
eager to explore them.

I went back to university to finish all my undergraduate studies and prepared from April to September 2013 for the National
Games, which are a must-do event for all the Chinese sports people.

On finishing my bachelor degree in Shanghai, I decided to do
a postgraduate degree in England. Many people asked me why I
chose to study in the UK rather than the US, which has the most
high-ranking universities. But I am very fond of Britain: the idyl-
lic countryside, the historical heritage, the friendly people, the
volunteering and charitable ethos and the rich sailing legacy.

At the end of 2013, I started to prepare for several exams in order to apply for the University of Southampton. I hoped to keep
doing some sailing while studying in the UK and Southampton
is surrounded by wonderful coastal venues, active sailing com-

munities as well as great maritime facilities.

To do this I needed to negotiate with my leaders from both the National and Shanghai team to get my private passport. (All Chinese athletes and officials working for the government use Public Affairs passports which cannot be used for personal purposes). But they wouldn't allow me to do anything other than staying in the team to train and sail all year round. I was threatened with the removal of all the money, honours and privileges I had for the rest of my life and they said that they wouldn't give me a good job after retirement. In other words: if I went against their orders (which were also the Communist Party's directives), I would have a miserable life in the future without their support.

In China, all the Olympic Champions are secured for life until the end of their days: assigned a top leadership job and career; granted a green channel for any medication requirements; awarded the highest subsidies and pension; and family members can share some of their supreme privileges as well. It is not true to say that I didn't care about losing these at all. But having the freedom to explore a life that I desire was far more important than that. I am prepared to experiment with a new life elsewhere if China really cut me off from everything.

In the end, I obtained my private passport by promising not to announce my retirement to the Chinese media so that the teams could still receive the funding and sponsorship which came from having world-class sailors in the team.

And so now I am studying at Southampton University in England.

If you asked me what the biggest challenge was for me about studying in the UK, I would reply without hesitation: 'critical thinking'. The British oriented critical methodology is very much a product of western culture, as I have discussed previously, stemming from Ancient Greek philosophy. You rigorously argue and defend each point of view and try to justify it objectively.

But critical thinking is not fostered or rewarded in most Asian countries. Our traditional beliefs, pursuing a state of harmony, strictly controlled and highly ordered communities discourage this. China-born and China-bred, we tend to lose the ability to think for ourselves and lack a vivid imagination.

Just raising your voice in front of people who are older than you is considered rude, let alone arguing with them! If you think the young have a different way of thinking, you'd better keep it to yourself rather than discussing with your elders. Otherwise what would come next would be a stream of endless criticism and you might get punished straight away.

The way we acquire knowledge is through a passive and stereotyped rote-learning, mostly by remembering and reciting. Hence the UK's different education system is an enormous transition for me and takes considerable time to learn and practise. The British university system is well respected throughout the world, and I truly appreciate the precious opportunity of studying in the UK and sincerely value the diversity of different cultures and religions. It is time to free my mind, let it fly and stimulate the creative opportunities which I missed in the past. Thinking critically can be both social and personal.

Living alone in a new country involves a huge amount of adaptation. But even so I can always feel the warmth of friendly people, enthusiasm of assistance offered, genuineness of communication, patience while explaining, understanding if conflicts occur, politeness under all circumstances, and the fresh air with blue skies.

The whole society shows no lack of individual caring. Maybe this is not so obvious to those living in Britain, but it is a lovely experience for me as a foreigner. The one-to-one tutorial system gives me personalised, in-depth, feedback as well as academic advice. Every assignment is returned with detailed remarks and suggestions. The university also provides me with Enabling Support Services to conquer the barriers from my hearing and eyesight deficiencies. The National Health Service (NHS) gave me a pair of customised hearing aids and with a pre-book system I no longer need to queue or squeeze through the crowds like in China. Socialising with people is such a pleasant experience that no one would force me to 'bottoms-up' any more. It's all about sincere communication and sharing wonderful ideas, stories or experiences. The air of democracy, fairness, equality and freedom of speech are all features I would never dare even dream of in China.

In the meantime, I hope I have also picked up some of the English courtesy. I understand that some of you feel uncomfortable whenever you see a Chinese person behaving badly. But please give them more understanding as they are utterly unaware of how unpleasant certain actions are to you. Many of your habits are not theirs. They would not consider, as you do, lowering their voice in public or on the phone, not making a sound when drinking, closing their mouth when chewing, never spitting directly onto the plate whilst eating, queueing in an orderly manner some distance from the person ahead, and many other things. Maybe the next time I go back to China I will notice the difference more after spending some time in England, just like you do.

Another aspect of the UK which impresses me is the general

ethos of volunteering. Sailing clubs are managed by volunteers; regattas are organised by volunteers; people deliberately put themselves out and make a huge effort to help those in need; there are plenty of charities as well as charitable shops. Parents also encourage their children to share and donate from a very early age. Shame on me that my parents taught me to be stingy and would not want to incur any losses. Even in recent years they would still try to keep things for themselves and become unhappy whenever they saw me sharing with other people.

Some say this 'Chinese' phenomenon was caused by extreme poverty in the past, especially for those who experienced the disastrous period which nearly cost them their lives. Others say it was caused by psychological factors because they had to keep fighting for things like food and property from the very beginning of their lives, and fear losing them again. Anyway, as the country improves, and from my generation onwards, people should become more loving and caring not only to their families and friends, but also expand this to the whole world.

Another subject one cannot avoid talking about is the British weather. Some may well complain how short the daylight is during winter time and how frequently it rains all year round. But doesn't it work well to stay warm indoors while the weather is cold and, by the time the warmer seasons come, you can do all kinds of activities outdoors as late as 10pm and still be in daylight? Well it is quite wet in the United Kingdom most of the time, but without it where would so much green, with a wide variety of grass, trees, forests, come from?

I easily 'survived' the British winter as most of the houses in Shanghai don't even have any radiators and imagine how cold it is to stay constantly around zero to five degrees for the whole day, whether indoors or out.

In general, I couldn't enjoy anything more than my life in Britain. But then what's next, after study? What is my future career likely to be? And where will I stay?

First, I would like to learn big boats (yachts, multihulls, foiling boats) as well as offshore sailing, both of which have much broader professional opportunities compared to the Olympic disciplines. But because China only focusses on Olympic development, with limited resources and experience, I barely know anything about sailing other than the ten Olympic classes. It was not until I spent more time abroad that I realised there were so many different types of sailboats and regattas which one can choose from: sailing for fun or racing competitively throughout one's life.

I hope that my Olympic experience is just a bright beginning to a lifelong sailing career. I hope that I can enjoy sailing offshore as much as I have enjoyed it inshore and can then train for my ultimate dream of sailing around the world. I know it would be intimidating at times, but I would also experience some breath-taking views which those on land would never see. However much of a challenge it would be, I would like to give it a try and hopefully my body would support me without too much pain in my joints due to frozen hands and feet in cold, wet and windy conditions.

I would also like to keep doing a few sailing events as a judge or umpire since I am very interested in rules and tactics. I have had the honour to learn from many leading 'rule makers and enforcers' throughout the world, who not only helped me throughout my Olympic campaigns, but also supported me in my journey to become a competent International Judge: Bill O'Hara from

Ireland, Bernard Bonneau from France, John Doerr and Ewan McEwan from the UK, Marianne Middelthon from Norway, Sofia Truchanowicz from Poland and many more. After working with them in events as well as meetings, I feel we sailors owe a lot to those volunteering professionals for their continuous hard work that keeps our sport a self-governing and yet joyous one.

Last, but not least, I would like to devote myself to promoting sailing in China and Asia. This sport is pretty developed in western countries but is only just beginning for those in the east. There is clearly a potential: China has such a long coastline – nearly twenty thousand miles; most Chinese people are no longer suffering poverty and have a better quality of life; dozens of new marinas are being built and hundreds of sailing clubs are being founded throughout the country. But it really needs more professionals, effective development systems, working with schools and making it available to all ordinary Chinese.

Here in Britain, the RYA (Royal Yachting Association) is the leading authority in sailing and cooperates with different organisations to promote this sport in general: providing schools and the youth the opportunities to experience sailing; supporting elite sailors campaigning for the Olympics; encouraging disabled people to be involved in this sport; designing and running high-standard qualifications and courses; working with the media to increase the coverage and image of water sports; publishing books for sharing knowledge and teaching maritime-related subjects; and ensuring safety while maximising enjoyment.

In this, the UK is a role model but in China we still have a long way to go. I will be most content if, by the end of my life, I can see the same depth in sailing all over China: a legacy for those future generations.

Chapter 21

Acknowledge the Cultural Differences

In this final chapter I want to highlight the cultural differences to help you understand the Chinese approach to life better. Personally I would highly recommend that you pay a visit to China if you haven't been there yet. The country has so much to offer as a travel destination, and you may well be intrigued by the very different lifestyle of people on the other side of the world. But before that, a little bit of background familiarisation to help you to have a deeper enjoyment of the exciting trip.

First of all, there are a few things that you need to bear in mind to avoid any shocking or unpleasant experiences before you hit the mainland of China.

Be prepared to see huge crowds of people (or 'mountain people mountain sea', as we say in China) when you are travelling in the centre of major cities like Beijing, Shanghai or Guangzhou. You may need to squeeze into the underground or buses at peak times if you are taking any public transport, otherwise you would never be able to get on board.

In the meantime, do take care of yourself and pay extra attention whenever you walk across the road, as in China it is the MIGHTY that is in the RIGHT! In other words, vehicles have the advantage over cyclists and them over the pedestrians.

176

While there are millions of people going to work by bike or moped, you will rarely see a single one use a helmet. The same with the Chinese sailing people, none of the RIB drivers bothered to use a kill cord, or wear a life jacket. It seems that the Chinese happily expose their lives to danger and hazards.

So do not assume that everybody will obey the traffic rules: it is always better to play it safe by observing the road carefully on both sides, especially since they drive on the opposite side to Britain. Furthermore, Chinese drivers learn and test their driving skills on specially designed and built obstacle courses. They would be granted the driving licence by passing a series of set manoeuvres around the course but having no real road practice or experience.

When you queue in China, try to stand close to the people in front of you, otherwise you will allow others to cut in. In the west the comfortable personal space is said to be around 45 cm whereas in China it is only 25 cm. To illustrate this, I had an embarrassing experience in the UK when I was once physically pushed by a lady ahead of me while queueing patiently, unaware of the narrow 'offensive' space I left between us.

Upon meeting a Chinese friend, a male may enthusiastically pass you a cigarette and then even offer to light it for you. Though it is illegal to smoke indoors in most places, this has very little effect. I suffered a lot in China through second-hand smoke and felt relieved after moving to England – never needing to suffer passive smoking any more indoors. So be prepared for this as well.

There may also be a few occasions that you see somebody spitting on the street with a loud, throat-clearing sound. Others might throw litter away anywhere but in the bin. You will also need to excuse some additional noises such as slurping soup (which is actually a good sign and an expression of delicious taste); and also foul-mouthed conversations in public, as if they were afraid that people in the vicinity couldn't hear them! I have the opposite problem in Britain due to my hearing. I find it very difficult to hear people and definitely need the hearing aids to help my understanding.

On the other hand, there are also some western habits which turn Chinese stomachs. Firstly, try not to blow your nose in public as it is deemed very disgusting. Next, avoid any extravagant body movement or exaggerated hand gestures while speaking which is fairly rude conduct in Chinese society. To give you another personal example, I always feel that the British are hyperactive when giving a presentation or making a speech. I wonder if a British person tries not to do a single movement, whether they would find it almost impossible to continue talking.

These, however, are just a reflection of our different culture, nothing to do with right or wrong, but acknowledging them will surely increase understanding between both countries.

Regarding the public facilities, one instance I would like to mention was actually commented on by some of my foreign friends who travelled to China. They said that it was the first time in their lives they had used a squat down toilet, but this is very common in all parts of the country. If this won't be an issue to you, then having some paper tissue at hand with you everywhere you go will definitely save you an awkward moment. The chances of no toilet paper are very high in most Chinese toilets. To be honest, I am still surprised that not a single toilet that I have been to in the UK so far has had no toilet paper: no matter how remote the place is or how poor the building looks. The

English are indeed much more civilised.

If you ask me whether Chinese people are friendly, my answer would be that it varies from place to place. However, as a foreigner in China, you would almost be treated like a celebrity: men and women may stare at you curiously; passers-by may want to take photos with you; strangers may point, talk about and smile at you, and so on. Try to get used to it as the Chinese are just inquisitive about westerners and their different appearance compared to Orientals.

On occasions when you are introduced to the Chinese, do not greet each other with kisses but only a few gentle handshakes. Most Chinese love career titles so try to replace their first name with the highest titles such as Professional Wang, Director Li, Doctor Ma, and so on. If you receive a gift, wait to open it privately when you get back to your room. This is opposite to the west where you would immediately open the gift in front of people.

In addition, be prepared to be asked some personal questions like what's your age, your job, height, weight; how much salary you earn; are you married, if not, why not; how many children you have, and many others. Don't be annoyed by this as these things are not deemed to be private to the Chinese and they are just trying to create a bond by showing they care through these enthusiastic conversations.

It is also the Chinese's habit to judge others' appearances openly, so they will say directly in front of you that you are very tall, you have a big nose, you are really handsome or beautiful, etc. Don't let these Chinese 'behaviours' upset you as they are not meant to offend you, instead take it easy and either answer honestly or refuse politely.

Anyway, there are many other infinitely exquisite Chinese customs waiting for you to find out for yourself. Remember the best strategy is always to maintain a sense of humour whenever something or someone strikes you as odd.

I have talked about the 'bottoms-up' drinking culture in China and, if you want to avoid getting drunk, then you need to be really firm and not be persuaded easily. Another amusing phenomenon after dining with Chinese friends is that they will 'fight' to pay the bill and never allow the others to share. There is no need to suggest everybody splits the bill, and let the Chinese pay if they insist over three times. In return you can prepare some gifts from your country as the Chinese are big fans of imported goods as they firmly believe anything made abroad will be better than those made in China. One tip here is to try to avoid clocks, umbrellas, handkerchiefs, shoes, candles, knives or mirrors as gifts as these are more or less related to separation and death to the Chinese.

Shopping in China may be a paradise or a nightmare. If you like fake luxury brands and pirated DVDs then you can easily spend days in some popular markets. However if you happen to be physically bigger than the average Chinese, then you might have trouble in finding suitable sizes in the shopping centre. I wear size 7 (40) shoes and the biggest women's size in most parts of China is 6 (38). I am also taller than many of the Chinese females and have wide shoulders. Consequently I would never fit into most womenswear even in size XL. As a result, I often ended up having no choice but to buy men's shoes and clothes. In contrast, this never troubles me when I shop in the UK as I only need to wear medium in ladies dresses and there are plenty of shoes in size 8 or 9. Phew...

If you stay in China for a longer period of time, there are so many wonderful things to learn from and explore in this ancient country: Tai Chi, Martial Arts or Kung Fu; Chinese pottery or calligraphy; delicious Chinese cooking and various regional cuisines; Chinese medicine such as herbal treatment, acupuncture, cupping, Chi Gong healing and foot or body massage; and best of all the language itself ranging from Mandarin and Cantonese to provincial vernaculars such as the Shanghainese I speak.

If you love singing, why not try out the many brilliant Karaoke studios (as far as I remember I seldom see any Karaoke in western countries, maybe a few in China Town). Also go ahead and experience the high-speed railway which can take you to almost any city and some large towns in China. Furthermore, the Maglev (magnetic levitation) in Shanghai gives you the unique experience of aeroplane speed travel on the ground. You cannot miss it as it runs from the Shanghai Pudong International Airport to the downtown area.

*

I hope you have enjoyed my stories and now have a better understanding of China. I love my country and respect what it is like to this day. Some of the problem 'issues' are just a product of a combination of history, tradition, culture and people. I genuinely wish in the near future that China can follow a healthier development, i.e. reduce the gap between the poor and the rich, have cleaner air quality with blue skies, generate a deeper moral caring attitude and cultivate more spiritual awareness. Whatever my future career will be and wherever I will be based in the long term, China will forever be my mother-nation and I cherish every link and opportunity between us.

A clear and useful message that I have learnt from my life experience so far is that every cloud has a silver lining. Behind all the barriers and obstacles there hides a bright turning point which you can only see or realise after a period of time. So many blessings in disguise are waiting for us to explore and discover, all we need is an optimistic attitude with our eyes wide open to see those little angels around us. Never ever give up as the time when you feel it is most difficult to continue is actually the golden moment to change your life and situation.

May you have a healthy, happy and loving life.

Achievements

Optimist class

1998	Chinese Championship	1st
1999	Asian Championship	1st
2001	World Championship	1st
2002	World Championship	1st
2002	Asian Games	1st

Europe class

2005	Chinese National Games	2nd

Laser Radial class

2005	ISAF Youth World Championship	2nd
2006	World Championship	1st
2006	Asian Games	1st
2008	World Championship	2nd
2008	Olympic Games	3rd
2009	Chinese National Games	1st
2012	World Championship	2nd
2012	Olympic Games	1st

On 25th November 2015 Lijia Xu announced that she will be campaigning for selection to represent China at the Rio 2016 Olympic Games

Bibliography

Ainslie, B., 2009. *Close to the Wind*. Yellow Jersey Press.

Anon, 2012. *The Secret Olympian*. Bloomsbury.

Bethwaite, F., 2008. *Higher Performance Sailing*. Adlard Coles Nautical.

Bassham, L. R., 1995. *With Winning in Mind: The Mental Management System*. BookPartners Inc.

Blackburn, M., 2001. *Sail Fitter: Sailing Fitness and Training*. Fitness Books.

Carmichael, C., 2004. *Chris Carmichael's Food for Fitness: Eat Right to Train Right*. Putnam Publishing Group, U.S.

Chang, J., 1991. *Wild Swans*. HarperCollins*Publishing*.

Emmett, J., 2011. *Be Your Own Tactics Coach*. John Wiley & Sons Ltd.

Emmett, J., 2015. *Coach Yourself to Win*. Fernhurst Books Limited.

Goodison, P., 2008. *RYA Laser Handbook*. The Royal Yachting Association.

Houghton, D. & Campbell, F., 2005. *Wind Strategy*. John Wiley & Sons Ltd.

Mujika, I., 2009. *Tapering and Peaking for Optimal Performance*. Human Kinetics.

Ostrowski, P. & Penner, G., 2009. *It's All Chinese to Me: An Overview of Culture & Etiquette in China*. Tuttle Publishing.

Verstegen, M., 2004. *Core Performance*. Rodale Inc.

Walker, S., 1986. *Advanced Racing Tactics*. W.W. Norton & Company Ltd.

Want Lily's success?

Follow in Lily's golden footsteps with tips, advice and challenging exercises from Lily's coach, **Jon Emmett**:

Coach Yourself to Win

Part of the iconic *Sail to Win* series, this book contains the twelve fundamental elements of successful sailing; a must-have for all sailors who aspire to great success. Foreword by Lijia Xu.

Be Your Own Tactics Coach

A comprehensive programme to make you a tactical genius; a practical way to improve your racing results, whether starting out, moving up the club circuit or competing at national level and beyond.

Published by Fernhurst Books

Making Waves

The real lives of sporting heroes on, in & under the water

A sneak peak of the second book in this series:

The First Indian
by Dilip Donde

1
A Path Less Travelled

"Dilip, are you in some sort of trouble with the Navy?" asked my mother one evening as we finished dinner at home in Port Blair. I had pushed away the empty dinner plate absentmindedly and was back to working on my laptop.

"What makes you think so?" I asked, trying to sound as nonchalant as possible while my brain was busy trying to word a suitable reply. The moment I had been apprehensive about for the past two months seemed to have arrived.

"Why have you suddenly started getting so many calls from Naval Headquarters, including the office of the Naval Chief? I think it is all very unusual so will you please tell me?" She had been staying with me for the past nine years and must have noticed the change in my routine since I got back from a sailing trip to Mumbai two months back. Through the years I had made it a point never to take any work home, howsoever busy the schedule. Since my return, however, I had been sitting almost every evening with a laptop borrowed from the office, reading up and writing well past midnight.

"I won't call it trouble but, yes, there is something I got myself into when I visited Mumbai for the sailing trip. I didn't tell you earlier as the whole thing still appears a bit harebrained and unrealistic to me," I mumbled, trying to find the right words to break the news and minimize any possible resistance.

"You can tell me whatever it is," persisted my mother.

"The Navy has been looking for someone to undertake a solo circumnavigation in a sailboat and I volunteered, though I am not exactly sure what it involves." I decided to play it straight, acutely aware of my terrible diplomatic skills, and waited for her reaction. The reaction was surprisingly positive, though not too unexpected.

"That is very good. Give it your best shot, opportunities like this don't come every day, but remember it is a one-way street!" she responded after a pause. "Don't ever think of backing out."

I decided to test her further by telling her that there was a good possibility that I may not come back alive from the trip. No Indian had undertaken such a trip, less than 200 in the world had been successful, and no one kept count of the unsuccessful attempts. That didn't deter her much as she calmly replied that I had to go some day like everyone else and it would be far better if I went trying to do something worthwhile! All she asked, in return of her full support, was to be able to read up as much as she could on the subject.

With her full support assured, I decided to fill her in on the events so far....

On 27 Apr 2006, before the start of the Mumbai to Kochi J 24 sailing rally that I was participating in, I met Capt Dhankhar, the Navy's Principal Director of Sports and Adventure Activities. Since he had flown down to flag off the rally along with the Chief of the Naval Staff, or CNS, the conversation was about ocean sailing in the Navy. As I escorted him to the Sailing Club moorings, he almost casually mentioned that the Navy was toying with the idea of sponsoring a solo circumnavigation by a naval officer.

"Can I be a part of it in some way?" I blurted out, stopping him in midsentence, throwing naval protocol to the winds. I just couldn't help it, the whole idea sounded so exciting though I had no clue what exactly was involved.

"Would you like to take it on? Should I tell the CNS that you have volunteered or do you need a little time to think about it?" he asked in his characteristic measured tone, with a hint of scepticism.

"Yes sir, please do tell the CNS that I want to volunteer, I don't need any time to think!" I replied, my brain in overdrive. Less than a minute back I was ready to play any part, howsoever small, in

this unknown project because it sounded interesting and suddenly the entire project seemed to be falling in my lap. I didn't bother to ask what exactly the Navy had in mind, all my fuzzy brain could sense was that this was something exciting and I shouldn't let go of the opportunity.

"Okay, now that you have volunteered, can you make a project report and send it to me by next month?"

In less than five minutes of what seemed like casual talk, I had gotten myself into the biggest soup in my life with a very vague idea about what exactly it was!

The Captain had been my instructor during my Clearance Diving course and had observed me closely during those stressful days. That, along with my declared enthusiasm for ocean sailing and my past experience as the Executive Officer of INS Tarangini during her first round the world voyage in 2002-2003, probably prompted him to check if I was interested in this project. Apparently I wasn't the first person he had asked but was definitely the first to fall for the idea, thus ending his search.

Later in the day, the CNS, Adm Arun Prakash, flagged off the rally. In his speech he declared that the Navy was ready to sponsor a solo circumnavigation under sail provided someone volunteered to take on the challenge. As we lined up for a group photograph, he approached and said, "Dilip, I heard you have volunteered!" I just nodded my head and murmured, " Yes sir. Let us see."

"So that is the story so far. Now I am required to make a detailed project report and send it to Naval Headquarters as of last month, which explains the frequent calls from Delhi. Honestly, I don't have a clue about the subject and have been trying to read about it on the Internet, which seems to be the only source of information here." I promised my mother that I would pass on whatever I read on the subject to her and got back to finalizing my report. Her unstinting support was a burden off my head. I didn't realize it then, but I had just conscripted the first member of the team for 'Sagar Parikrama', as the project would be called.

More than a month went by and I still hadn't submitted my project report. One reason was a fairly busy work schedule that allowed me to read up on the subject only after dinner at home; the other, a total lack of knowledge about the subject. It would be an understatement to say that I was groping in the dark. The more I started reading, the more I started realizing that this was not something romantic and poetic as I had initially thought but would involve a lot of hard work and would be far more difficult than what I had imagined. Surprisingly, though, that increased my excitement and determination to make it happen.

By Jul 2006, I managed to submit my project report to Naval Headquarters (NHQ) and decided that if I had to do a circumnavigation it had to be a proper circumnavigation under sail, going through the Southern Ocean, round the three Great Capes, Cape Leeuwin, Cape Horn and the Cape of Good Hope. I could have proposed following the route taken by the previous Indian sailing expeditions in *Trishna*, *Samudra* and INS

Tarangini through the Suez and Panama canals, called it a circumnavigation and no one would have been wiser, in the country at least! In fact, on hindsight, things would have turned out to be much simpler as I could always have pointed at 'precedence', something that opens many a door when dealing with the bureaucracy. I could have had a whale of a time stopping at 40 to 50 ports over a period of a year or two with a smooth sail through the Trade Winds! But then that wouldn't have been the real thing. Even if the Navy, and the taxpayer who was essentially funding my trip, didn't realize it, I would, and it just would not be right!

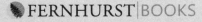
FERNHURST|BOOKS

Find out more at **www.fernhurstbooks.com**